The Presidents' Doctor

The Presidents' Doctor

An Insider's View of
Three First Families

Milton F. Heller, Jr.

VANTAGE PRESS
New York

For

Helen Koch Boone,

whose love, wisdom, and keen sense of humor
made a great career possible

Contents

Illustrations

(In chronological order. Unless a note accompanying an illustration indicates otherwise, the Boone Collection is the source.)

Preface

No one was better acquainted with the personalities—one might even say White House secrets—of the administrations of the three presidents of the United States during the 1920s, Warren G. Harding, Calvin Coolidge, and Herbert Hoover, as was the late Dr. Joel T. Boone. He was assistant White House physician during the first two administrations, physician during the last. In all three, as well in the early days of the Franklin D. Roosevelt administration, Boone was a figure of importance, in a position to know a great deal. By the end of his life, he could count nine presidents—Harding through Nixon—as friends.

Boone kept voluminous notes and collected a mass of documents, photographs, and newspaper clippings. In later years, after retirement from the U.S. Navy as a vice admiral, full of honors, winner of the Congressional Medal of Honor in World War I, medical officer for the Third Fleet in World War II, head of veterans' hospitals throughout the country, Admiral Boone organized his material as a huge autobiographical account that told a great deal about his closeness to the administrations of the 1920s, together with all the other experiences of his long life.

Boone was born and brought up in the anthracite coal region of Pennsylvania, where his father was a feed merchant. Upon graduation from Mercersburg Academy and the Hahnemann Medical College in Philadelphia he joined the navy and served with the Marines in Haiti and then in 1918 with the Second Division in France. He began his tour with the presidents in 1922 as physician on the presidential yacht *Mayflower*, soon became part of the White House medical team, and continued duty there until two months into the FDR administration. Thereafter Boone served at sea and ashore in various capacities. At the end of World War II he was the first person to go ashore in the Tokyo Bay area, where, characteristically, he sought out and found many hundreds of neglected, war-weary U.S. and other Allied prisoners. During the administration of Pres. Harry S. Truman, Boone led a historic medical survey of the bituminous coal industry and then became chief medical director of the Veterans Administration.

This extraordinary physician-officer was a mixture of traits not usually found in the services. He was a maverick, who did not consider himself a maverick because he usually adhered to convention, dressing immaculately, paying attention to the navy's and society's protocols, applying strict moral and ethical standards to himself as well as others. He did not look the part, as he was a mere five-six, but behind his open countenance was a mind that sought to make sense out of every situation he encountered, and if it did not make sense he said so. His independence caused him to risk confrontations that other officers would have sidestepped. And there was another notable characteristic. He considered himself on an equal footing with line officers and on occasion fought as one of them, ignoring the tradition of subservience associated with the role of a staff officer.

Boone's life spanned many changes. In childhood he had heard the tales of naval prowess at Santiago Bay. He himself participated in the two great world wars. Thereafter he could watch the navy going nuclear, an impossible dream in 1898. In old age, compiling his memoirs, upon which the pages that follow draw in detail, he could survey his life from an era when the navy took on proportions never imagined by such earlier individuals as John Paul Jones, nor, for that matter, by Jones's contemporary in the then western wilderness of Kentucky, the irrepressible Daniel Boone, Joel Boone's distant cousin.

Acknowledgments

Heartfelt thanks are due to many people for their assistance in bringing this book to fruition. Aware of the many years her father had devoted to collecting material and preparing to write his life story, my late wife, Suzanne, after Dr. Boone's death urged me to continue the work that had been so important to him. As one who had the run of the White House during childhood, she offered an unusual perspective on the First Families. She also provided useful insight to her father as a physician whose dedication to his country and to serving his illustrious patients was so intense that scant time was available for his own little family.

Following Suzanne's untimely death, family members and friends assisted in reading and editing manuscript draft, for which I am thankful. I am especially grateful to my wife, Marion, for the endless hours she has contributed to the project and to my son "Mickey" (Milton F. Heller III) for his research assistance. My brother-in-law, Vice Admiral E. P. (Dennis) Wilkinson, U.S. Navy (Ret.), served as an invaluable critic of the work.

Two eminent historian/authors to whom I am heavily indebted are Dr. Robert H. Ferrell, Distinguished Professor of History Emeritus at Indiana University in Bloomington, and Mr. Jan K. Herman, U.S. Navy Medical Department Historian and editor of *Navy Medicine* magazine. Over the years, these gentlemen have given generously of their time and talent in editing and offering suggestions on the content, presentation, and publication of the manuscript. Their combined knowledge of the major subjects of this book—lives of U.S. presidents and the history and practice of navy medicine—along with their extensive writing experience proved to be invaluable resources. Many thanks to both Bob and Jan.

1

Early Years

Joel Thompson Boone, descended from a long line of Quakers, became a man with the courage to stand up for his principles—whether in opposition to an immediate superior, a national figure, or an enemy on the battlefield.

Born on August 29, 1889, in a small Pennsylvania town named St. Clair, young Boone was a shy lad, perhaps because of his Quaker background and most certainly in part as a result of the loss of his mother at an early age and the domination thereafter by an oppressive father. One of his early memories was at age eleven when with his brother and two sisters he stood in front of the family's modest house and waved good-bye to his mother, who was journeying off to Philadelphia, there to be operated on for cervical cancer. Not long after, having suffered the operation, she died.

Life in those early years was difficult. Boone's father kept stables as part of his hay and grain business, and the son's task was to help with all the drudgery involved with them, which meant work from morning till night, save for time spent in school. The lad received nothing in return except what might be described as maintenance, which was a cold-plate supper each night. A horsewhip was always nearby. The father was a heavy drinker, according to some family members. Life was not made any easier when he remarried, for the presence of a stepmother is seldom easy and in Boone's case the remarriage meant arrival in the household of the stepmother's mean-spirited daughter.

School became a sort of salvation for the youngster, and gradually life became easier. After two years at Pottsville High School, his stepmother, of all people, suggested that he spend his senior year at a nearby private school, Mercersburg Academy

As a three-year-old

As a teen-ager driving his father's delivery wagon

destined to become one of the best-known "prep" schools in the eastern United States. In those days it was a Spartan place with just a few buildings. But the educational arrangements were first-class; students received real attention. A year in this fine school made a large difference in Boone's mental outlook. At the beginning, when called upon to represent the "new boys" in addressing a large group, he was so bashful that he found it impossible to speak. But excellent guidance and participation in a variety of activities such as debating and track events served to broaden his horizons and make him a little more self-confident.

Mercersburg would constitute one of the most formative experiences in Boone's life. He never forgot it, remembering appreciatively fellow students, the teachers he so admired, and, of course, the exhilaration of academic courses and their athletic accompaniments. Over the years, he would demonstrate his devotion to the school through financial contributions he could ill afford, through service as head of alumni and trustees, and by assisting in enrollment of two sons and a nephew of presidents of the United States. The school reciprocated by naming a large new building for him.

In Boone's youth two other influences made their appearance. One was a young lady whom he had first met when he was ten years old, Helen Elizabeth Koch, who appeared at the birthday party of one of his teenage sisters. He could hardly believe his eyes when he espied the pretty brunette daughter of a judge in nearby Pottsville. Love, one should add, was not a part of this first vision of Helen, who would become Boone's wife. At the outset she was only a friend of his sister. In high school Helen acquired more importance. She was an excellent student, popular with schoolmates. She played the piano for the class's daily singing, and Boone thought that while she was playing, apparently looking at the music on the rack, she was peering through the rack at him—which actually was the case. Their relationship soon was flourishing, and like many turn-of-the-century romances, it was nourished by activities that would not have seemed stirring or even worthwhile in any way to later teenagers accustomed to more exciting ventures. Joel and Helen spent their spare time sleigh and hay riding, picnicking, dancing, swimming, and boating.

The other influence on Boone's future years was his uncle, Dr. George Boone. Joel rode in the buggy with Dr. Boone during his trips around St. Clair and the countryside when the physician treated patients and delivered babies in their homes, a custom now forgotten, nearly impossible to imagine in an era when people go to the doctor rather than the latter going to them. Boone watched all this activity with interest, even fascination.

After the year at Mercersburg and graduation, the question arose of what to do next; here the experience with Uncle George led Boone into medicine. How did youths at the turn of the century prepare for a medical career? High school, a short experience of two or three years, was an innovation of only a generation earlier. Previously, young people seldom went beyond grade school, ending their educations at grade six. Even at the turn of the century Boone was fortunate to have completed high school. After graduation at sixteen or seventeen, young men specialized in medicine immediately, without three or four years of work in a college or university. And so it was not merely possible but quite ordinary for someone like Joel Boone to leave Mercersburg and go immediately to medical school, which in his case was Hahnemann Medical College in Philadelphia.

Hahnemann made a lasting impression. One day, while conversing with a professor, the young man had quite a shock. The doctor unburdened himself by admitting that he was the one who had operated on Boone's mother and had always felt it was his error in changing the procedure during the operation that caused her to die from shock and loss of blood. As much as he had grieved over his mother, Boone could not help but admire the professor's admission of a fatal mistake. How many physicians today, fearing a malpractice suit, would risk being so forthright?

At Hahnemann, Boone admired a skilled professor of surgery, William B. Van Lennep, who in those early days of appendectomies could locate with great dexterity a hidden or abnormally placed appendix. At a time when huge carbuncles on the back of the neck were common, this surgeon made a radical incision and burned out the area with a long, wide soldering iron.

5

As the iron was applied, a stench of burning flesh permeated the amphitheater where he operated.

It was Boone's good fortune to be selected to serve as one of Van Lennep's assistants during the summer between the junior and senior years. One of his duties during evening hours was to make out bills, standing in the office at a wall desk while the professor sat behind a floor desk. Reminded of operations, Dr. Van Lennep would stipulate what to charge a particular patient. Boone remembered one answer: "She has six children; her husband has left her. Even though it was a very long and complicated operation, send her a receipted bill." Boone's next query concerned a patient on whom a simple appendectomy had been performed. This time he said, "That is that very rich bachelor who lives at the Union League. Send him a bill for one thousand dollars."[1]

During the summer with Dr. Van Lennep, Boone practiced obstetrics in Philadelphia's slums. It was an unusual experience, since the medical student was on his own and had to face unexpected situations in dangerous parts of the city. Boone recalled that one day as he was about to leave Van Lennep's house in response to a call from a patient in labor, he reached into a vase and put a yellow chrysanthemum in his buttonhole; boutonnieres were popular in those days. Entering the patient's fourth-floor apartment, he found the huge husband drunk from celebrating in advance the arrival of the child. As Boone went about his work, the man staggered around the bedroom and swore, urging the mild-mannered little woman, who already had six children, to get on with it. After delivering a baby boy, Boone started down the three flights. A heavy hand reached over the balustrade and seized him by the shoulder. It was the husband, who pulled the chrysanthemum from the lapel and ground it into the floor. In brogue he shouted a profanity followed by, "Don't you know it's Orangemen's Day?"[2] With that, he pushed Boone down the stairs.

There were times when Boone was accosted by prostitutes. On one occasion when the figure emerging from the darkness saw the medicine bag she retreated, saying "Excuse me, doctor."[3] Here was a whore with manners, Boone thought.

Upon graduation there was a one-year internship at Hahnemann, where Boone spent time in the emergency ward. The hospital was near police and fire stations and handled a heavy volume of accident cases. Often he followed the horse-drawn fire engines as they rushed through the streets, bells clanging and engines smoking. There was a sordid part in the work: police swept intoxicated people off the streets in early-morning hours, and after Boone treated them he placed them on iron cots with oilcloth-covered mattresses in a basement room to "sleep it off."

1

Life passed in a rush until the internship came to an end and Dr. Joel T. Boone had to decide what to do next. "Next" proved a berth, so to speak, in the U.S. Navy. This turn resulted from a dinner that he and his fiancée, Helen, had with his distant relative Uncle Charlie Dyson, a captain in the navy. Dyson told him there were doctors in the navy and that the navy paid regularly. This was not insignificant for a young physician in the early years of the twentieth century when physicians' incomes were small. It was only later, following World War II, that doctors' incomes turned upward. Helen was adamantly opposed to the navy, even though a pay check would facilitate early marriage. But once Boone's interest had been piqued, he pursued and obtained a commission. He married Helen Koch on June 20, 1914.

Even after being commissioned in the navy, Boone was easily embarrassed. Upon reporting to the commanding officer at his first duty station, the Portsmouth Naval Hospital in New Hampshire, he stumbled over his sword, which had been put on backward. After apologizing for that blunder, his face again turned red when the commanding officer asked him to remove his cap while in the office. In Portsmouth, Boone was overwhelmed by the responsibilities thrust upon him. As one of three medical officers he was chief of medicine, chief of neuropsychiatry, and assistant in the department of surgery. A few weeks later he learned that he was also the pathologist.

The shock of this first duty in the United States Navy was not eased by the hospital's head, Commander Frederick William

With bride in Atlantic City

Ferdinand Wieber, a native of Germany. Dr. Wieber had not lost his accent or mannerisms. When war broke out in Europe his overriding concern was for relatives serving in the German army and navy, and he spent most of the day reading news of the war. He left Boone to sink or swim.

Helen was at Joel's side to help him adjust to the navy's unfamiliar ways. As in years to follow, she sacrificed material comforts in the interest of his career. The quarters the young couple occupied in Portsmouth and other places were crude. In one place they lived in a tiny back room of a third-floor walkup, lighted by a squirting gas jet; in another, bathroom facilities consisted of an outhouse in the garden. Money for entertainment was meager. A bicycle served as transportation.

After two months in Portsmouth, Boone was ordered to the Naval Medical School in Washington, D.C., where upon completion of the course he received a commission in the regular navy; up to that time he had been serving in the reserve. From Washington, he and Helen went to Norfolk, where Boone expected to go to sea. He had not expressed any preference for duty but declared to Helen that he did not want to go to Haiti, where the United States recently had sent marines to quell an uprising. One day, upon returning from a ride in their newly acquired automobile, a friction-drive four-cylinder Metz, Helen and Joel found a telegram from the Navy Department under their rooming house door. It was orders to proceed to Annapolis and report to the marine barracks for duty in Haiti.

From the deck of the USS *Tennessee*, the first view of Haiti was startlingly magnificent. The sapphire blue sea contrasted with towering mountains from the water's edge up through clear blue skies to a high layer of fleecy white clouds. The enchantment was short-lived. Up close, the sights in Port-au-Prince, where the marines landed, were horrible, with filth, congestion, and poverty. Adults and children relieved themselves on the sidewalks, gutters, and streets, even amid produce for sale in the marketplace. Flies and other insects infested both excrement and food.

In these surroundings, Boone was expected not only to hold sick call for the marines, the native police, and native prisoners

As a young lieutenant (j.g.)

In front of dispensary in Haiti

11

but to introduce rudimentary sanitation as well.

The poor element of the native population was deprived of medical attention of any kind; local physicians, most of them educated in France, demanded payment in cash before they would treat anyone, even in an emergency. Medical and surgical facilities were crude. When Boone was called upon to amputate the leg of a boy whose foot had been crushed under a train, he had only a wooden table on which to operate, a kerosene lamp for illumination, and chloroform as an anesthetic.

After a few weeks in Port-au-Prince, he was transferred to the First Regiment at Cap Haïtien, which lies across the northern peninsula from Port-au-Prince. The native Caco outlaws had been attacking the marines in that area. Afterward, he was ordered on a five-day expedition with fifty marines and two officers. This was initiation to sleeping on the ground with a rock for a pillow and the heavens for protection. He recalled arising in the morning wringing wet from the dew, covered with ants and mosquitoes as large as horseflies.

The expedition traversed revolutionary country without incident, although it did run across several "generals" regarded as gang leaders. One was taken as a guide, with the thought that he would offer protection from treachery on the part of his compatriots.

Just a week after this first field experience, Boone rejoined the artillery battalion (Thirteenth Company) at Grand Rivière, a small place fifteen miles inland from Cap Haïtien. There he participated in forays into the country. His company's instructions were to disarm the Cacos and destroy their forts, many of which could be approached only over twisting and precipitous trails. In searching for Cacos over a four-week period Boone walked perhaps 450 miles. Cacos were like mosquitoes hidden away in vegetation or trees and in bare feet would approach without a sound. As they came out of hiding they swung their machetes, decapitating victims.

The first serious attack on Fort Rivière took place on October 29, 1915, with 133 marines assisted by a pack train of twenty mules and twelve horses marching and fighting continuously for twenty-one and one-half hours, from 4:00 A.M. on the first day to

1:30 A.M. the next. The fort was at the top of a four-thousand-foot ridge and could be approached by a two-foot-wide trail that rose almost perpendicularly through a canyon. Under fire from the Cacos, who held five mountain peaks, the marines suffered, with heat, altitude, and severity of the climb taking their toll. Boone prodded the men with a combination of encouragement and curses. Bringing up machine guns, the men scaled the last peak and drove the Cacos away.

Unfortunately, the Cacos reoccupied the fort, for the marines had failed to destroy it. A second attack took place on November 17 and proved the most difficult action the marines had participated in since the Civil War. The attack was to be from four directions, simultaneously at 8:00 A.M. Maj. Smedley D. Butler's Fifth Company began firing from west of the mountain range fifteen minutes before the appointed time. The other columns opened up, and with all approaches and apparent means of escape for the Cacos covered, the marines charged. Butler and his troops approached over an open plain, while the Thirteenth Company had to go down a mountain into a ravine and up a hill beneath the fort while exposed to heavy fire.

As machine guns swept the fort, the troops spread and climbed as fast as possible, yelling all the way. When C. C. Campbell, captain of the Twenty-third Company, saw the Cacos emerging from a breach in the fort's wall and jumping into a dried-up moat and that his lieutenants were busy elsewhere, he shouted to Boone to go after them. Boone took six marines and headed toward the hole. The climb was steep and the men exhausted, but Boone kept them moving.

Boone was anxious that his group be first to enter the fort. He pushed two men into the moat, and from there they shot Cacos as they fell over the wall. One of the marines was boosted as he stood on a rifle held by three others. He reached down and with help of a rifle pulled up each of the others. From there Boone's band jumped into the fort, shouting "Thirteenth Company!" so other marines would not mistake them for Cacos.

Hand-to-hand combat commenced, with the marines shooting, bayoneting, and smashing Caco skulls with rifle butts. Suddenly they heard someone shout, "Who the hell are you?"[4] It was

Celebrating capture of Fort Rivière in Haiti

14

Major Butler, with his men. The meeting raised a question as to who had entered the fort first. In any case, the battle had given Boone an opportunity to lead men in combat—a unique experience for a physician, even one in the armed service.

A few weeks after Fort Rivière, Boone went to Port-au-Prince and thence to Jérémie, due west near the tip of the southern peninsula. There he made friends, including a German pharmacist, Dr. Kuhn, who had been in Haiti for twenty-three years. Kuhn lived with a black woman, explaining it by saying, "When in Rome, do as the Romans do!"[5] Boone had long conversations with Kuhn on a variety of subjects, but whenever he asked about the military situation in Europe the pharmacist would clam up. After Boone returned to the United States, he learned that Kuhn had been a reservist in the German army.

In Jérémie, Boone found rampant graft. Inspecting the prison, he learned that the jailer was extracting fifty cents from each prisoner due to be released and if the prisoner refused to pay he would be kept locked up. Judges, district attorneys, and political leaders all lived on graft. But the town offered one advantage. There Helen could join Joel. Unfortunately, he overslept on the very morning of Helen's arrival on the *Columbia* and did not awaken until he heard blasts from the ship's whistle signifying desire for clearance by the port doctor as a requisite to landing. Since the doctor was none other than Boone, he dressed posthaste and rushed to the dock where the native port officer and oarsmen dressed in khaki uniforms newly made for the occasion waited to row him in style. After greeting Helen and completing the inspection, he and his wife breakfasted and were rowed back to the dock.

Since the receding tide had widened the gap between the small boat and the first step on the dock, the port officer offered his hand to Helen. She took it and stepped onto the dock. Helen was the first American woman to live in Jérémie. Since residents had heard of racial prejudice in the United States they had been curious to see whether she would take the man's hand. They came in droves to witness her arrival. As she and Joel were driven from the dock in a carriage up the main street toward their house in the country, people rushed onto balconies and cheered. Later, when children in the streets saw her riding the bay Joel had bought for her, they would call, "Garde, garde, petit garçon!"[6] Helen did not mind being described as a little boy, since she realized that with breeches and astride the horse she was departing from local custom of ladies riding side-saddle.

Soon after Helen's arrival, the Boones began Saturday-afternoon receptions. They entertained nursing sisters one Saturday, French brothers another. Boone went out of his way to buy prunelle liqueur from Dr. Kuhn for the brothers, although when the time came to make a toast the first swallow set his throat on fire.

During the months in Jérémie, Boone accompanied the marine paymaster on trips into the backcountry by boat or horseback. The trips were not pleasant, as revealed by comments in Boone's diary: "The French serve too much wine for comfortable traveling . . . Paid the people and turned in after a rotten supper . . . Had lunch with the Mayor—garlic and grease . . . Roads very rough and mountainous . . . Disgusted with that way of traveling . . . Mosquitoes very bad and interfering with my sleep."[7] A few days after a trip he came down with what was diagnosed as estivo-autumnal malaria, a malignant form, with high fever, horrible headaches, body aches, and nausea. The quinine he had been taking ever since arriving proved ineffective. He was removed by tug to the field hospital in Port-au-Prince, arriving June 20, his second wedding anniversary. He said later he had no recollection of the journey.

The hospital experience was unforgettable.

I was given a very large dose—I think they said 500cc of quinine solution, from which I had a very severe circulatory collapse. I remember lying . . . semiconscious, ceased to be able to feel the cot under me, and then I felt that I was floating off into space . . . I was losing consciousness and likely dying. Doctor Williams . . . felt my pulse and he said, "My God! Get me camphorated oil immediately!" The corpsman returned to say that they had no camphorated oil . . . and the doctor said excitedly: "For God's sake, get me some ether, bring me several hypodermics of ether! I want . . . Boone's dying; I can't get his pulse at all now. I could a little bit ago." I opened my eyes with great effort . . . saying, "Please

16

do all you can for me," and passed into unconsciousness again. I understood that I was given several hypodermic injections of ether, which served to restore my circulation."[8]

From Port-au-Prince he was transferred to the USS *Solace*, a hospital ship, and Helen was left to her own devices to make her way back to the United States. In Haiti, Boone had the first of many experiences on the battlefield. It was here also that he first encountered serious illness, a challenge he was to face and overcome time and again.

2

After the duty in Haiti there followed, within the next half-dozen years, an extraordinary series of assignments, some of which must be passed over hurriedly, despite their interest to Boone and their very real interest to any reader today. At the outset, for example, the doctor was assigned to the battleship *Wyoming* where he came under the stern eye of Capt. Henry A. Wiley, later the well-known admiral. Despite baptism in fire in Haiti, Boone was still a shy person. He recounts that as the most junior officer he found it difficult to make conversation with fellow members of the *Wyoming*'s wardroom mess, even staying away from meals if he heard that strangers might be present as guests.

Then within a year he was on the way to France as a battalion surgeon with the marine brigade of the U.S. Second Division, unique as a hybrid of army, navy, and Marine Corps personnel. The crossing in the new *Henderson*—a ship Boone was to encounter later, under memorable circumstances—was miserable because of rough seas, heavy rain, and shortage of bunks. Upon landing with his medical contingent lined up on the dock, Boone had a feeling there were serious errors in the choice of personnel, for the men were as green as grass and some were such poor physical specimens as to be unfit. He was to find out otherwise, but the moment was hardly reassuring.

Next he was sent to infantry school at Gondrecourt as a result of a bureaucratic error; it should have been sanitary school. At the end of that experience Boone came down with influenza and was hospitalized for twenty-three days. Upon recovery there was training with the regiment in a quiet sector of the front in the Vosges Mountains. The experience was unpromising, for night after night in below-freezing temperatures he stood with troops in the mud. Despite a fine knitted helmet worn under the steel helmet to cover face and neck, with wristlets, two pairs of stockings, hobnailed shoes, woolen gloves, and a trench coat, he was cold.

After that Boone attended an army sanitary school at Langres, with visits to clinics and hospitals in Paris, also to a tour of a sector of the British front where he heard the announcement, "Breakfast is at seven, lunch at one, tea at four-thirty, and dinner at eight."

In April 1918, he went to Verdun to rejoin the Sixth Marines as assistant regimental surgeon. The trench warfare at Verdun was of course continuous, as the trenches outside the city had been places of terrible slaughter in 1916. Here Boone carried a cane made of a steel rod covered with woven reed and with a sharp point that could save his life in a surprise encounter with the enemy.

Not long afterward, the Sixth Regiment and the rest of the brigade, indeed the entire division, were thrown into a gap in the French lines at a place that became famous in American military history, Belleau Wood. The Germans were about to break through for Paris. Matters were so serious that trucks stood outside the American embassy and other offices in the city, ready for evacuation. In a long line of trucks, the Americans, many of them singing as they rode, moved up to the front. The divisional commander had no idea where the Germans were and simply flung his men to right and left, a brigade on either side of the Paris road, stretching out as far as they could.

Studying maps and talking with Col. Albertus W. Catlin and Lt. Comdr. Wray G. Farwell, the regimental commander and surgeon, Boone decided the best place for a dressing station would be a farm named Petit Montgivault that he had noticed before entering Lucy-le-Bocage. He and his corpsmen found the farmhouse occupied by an elderly couple. They proceeded to

In front of dugout at Verdun

With motorcycle and sidecar at Verdun

set up a dressing station for wounded at an end of the barn where hay was stored and another station at the other end toward the orchard. Under the barn Boone found an empty wine cellar that he felt could be useful if artillery fire became intense, especially at night when no lights were to be shown.

He stood behind a hedge in the orchard and looked across the plowed fields. From there, Boone watched the brigade go on the attack on June 6 at 5:00 P.M. Suddenly he saw one of his corpsmen, Oscar Goodwin, come running up from the ravine into the orchard, seize a stretcher, and—still on the run—disappear into the waving wheat. Goodwin made four trips through machine-gun fire to save a single albeit important wounded man—Colonel Catlin. The colonel had made the error of standing up in a trench, offering a target for a sniper who shot him through the chest.

This was only the first of many courageous acts Goodwin performed, and Boone repeatedly recommended him for awards. A friendship developed, and with Boone's help Goodwin later attended medical school and took up practice in his native North Carolina.

Petit Montgivault proved ideal for a station, for it was off the Paris–Metz highway at the point of a triangle formed by Lucy, Belleau Wood, and Bouresches. Through the night of June 6, it received the wounded, French as well as marine, as the battle raged and French forces moved through U.S. lines. Most casualties were from rifle fire, machines guns, and shells, although some were from gas and grenades.

From the lines the wounded usually passed to a battalion aid station that might be a cellar, dugout, cave, culvert, ravine, gutter, wooded area, stone wall, even an open field—any place offering protection. From there they went up the ravine to a culvert under the road from Lucy to Bouresches. There, in a small space, with protection of a stone wall that supported the road overhead and of the sidewalls, Boone and his men collected casualties on straw bedding before moving them into the dressing station. After the war the assistant divisional surgeon, Richard Derby, son-in-law of former president Theodore Roosevelt, told of a visit to Petit Montgivault:

21

Culvert used as a dressing station at Belleau Wood (Reproduced from
the collections of the Library of Congress)

Passing through several overlapping ponchos hung in the doorway to conceal the interior lighting, I was at first blinded, and I mean this literally, by the bright candle-light from within. The small room was the scene of intense activity. Two litter racks occupied the central floor space . . . supporting a wounded man who was being worked over by a medical officer and several hospital corpsmen. Clamps had just been applied to the divided brachial artery in a badly wounded upper arm, and the tourniquet was being loosened but left in place to guard against accident during his subsequent evacuation. . . . Captain Boone was directing the dressings and evacuations with great speed and skill. . . . These were the days in which men worked until they dropped and then rose to work again.[9]

In absence of a table of any kind, limbs were amputated right on the floor. Patients were treated with doses of morphine and warmed in blankets with help of a small alcohol stove. The station was known as the ambulance head, since it was impossible for ambulances to go beyond toward the front, not even into Lucy. Often there were as many as twenty-five at the station. Having been shot at so much, and with almost every inch of ground peppered, the medical people at Petit Montgivault believed a lucky horseshoe must be suspended from the sky.

Treating hundreds of wounded, they accumulated a large pile of rifles, helmets, bandoliers, and other gear in the courtyard. Along with the coming and going of ambulances and food carts, this caught the attention of German aviators, who directed fire against it. On June 9 the barn took a direct hit, which removed much of the roof and part of the walls. Boone concluded that someone must have cut the string that held the horseshoe.

Lack of antibiotics and plasma was a serious problem and the cause of thousands of American, not to mention Allied, deaths. Dakin-Carrel therapy, involving continuous irrigation of wounds with a nonirritating antiseptic fluid carried by rubber tubes, was introduced early in the war and was found to be effective, even for obstinate infections. Bacteria could not live in the fluid. Supplies were limited and treatment could not be in the front lines.

23

A treatment devised for burns was more available at the front. It consisted of coating or spraying the denuded surface of the body with melted paraffin, covering it with a thin layer of cotton batting, and sealing the whole with another layer of paraffin. The hardened paraffin formed an air-tight envelope that gave the patient some comfort and served as a scaffolding under which skin could grow from the edges and cover the raw surface.

Wounds almost always became infected from dirty clothing and from the soil of France contaminated with manure and the tetanus organism. Antitetanus injections therefore were routine.

There was inordinate loss of human limbs because in dealing with a mangled arm or leg there was no alternative to amputation. Extensive debridement of wounds was performed at the dressing station, with bruised and devitalized tissue and bone radically excised. Control of hemorrhage by tourniquet and treatment of shock by morphine and heat were also common procedures.

Chest wounds presented a problem, but early in American participation in the war an enterprising corpsman hit on the idea of pinning together, with a safety pin, the skin and subcutaneous tissues of a gaping chest wound, keeping air out. Surprisingly this crude procedure proved so successful it was widely adopted, saving many lives.

Toward the end of the fighting, illness became a more severe problem than wounds. From the Second Division as many as five hundred officers and men were evacuated each day, one in five being battle casualties. Boone suffered a gastrointestinal infection that plagued him all the way to Germany. His condition was so bad that when the advance halted at Fosse for several days he was leaving his quarters day and night to go out into the fields. He already had been suffering from repeated poison gas attacks. He weakened and his weight went down to 110 pounds.

Upon recommendation of the regimental, brigade, and division commanders, Boone was awarded the army's Distinguished Service Cross for "extraordinary heroism in the Bois de Belleau."

Following Belleau Wood and a few days in the Marne Valley the regiment proceeded to what everyone thought was a rest area near Paris. On the night of July 16–17 a change of orders turned everyone around, and after an all-night rough ride in an ammunition truck, in a caravan that stretched for miles, Boone found himself in a woods, Villers Cotterêts, fifteen miles southwest of Soissons. He was about to take part in the Soissons offensive to push in a salient that stretched into Allied lines. Once again the Second Division, together with other U.S. divisions, was being thrown in. Villers Cotterêts was in a state of chaos, the road packed with guns, trucks, ambulances, and humanity. Stumbling through woods in the night, July 17–18, officers and men lost their units. Food and shelter were short.

The attack at Soissons was unforgettable. Lying in mud, Boone heard all hell break loose at 4:30 A.M. on July 18. Thousands of artillery pieces, packed together along a thirty-five-mile front, poured forth a rolling barrage that made him shudder. Shells clipped trees with a rain of branches and tree trunks that decapitated men below. Everyone sought shelter, clawing with hands, bayonet, or trench shovel to make any sort of hole. Boone remembered asking a chief pharmacist's mate—a tall, unkempt, raw-boned, droll fellow named Whittaker—how he found protection. "Hell, I jumped into a trench, and it was warm," was the response. "I got as low down into it as I possibly could to protect myself, to discover afterwards that I had jumped into a field latrine which had been used over a long period of time, apparently."[10]

The Second Division suffered hundreds of casualties, and to care for the wounded Boone and corpsmen took over a huge cave recently abandoned by the Germans. This crude shelter was destined to accommodate 350 men at a time. It was here that fragments from a bursting shell struck a wounded soldier Boone was treating and knocked down so much dirt and rocks that Boone was nearly buried alive. A corpsman rushed out of the cave and extricated him.

Soon thereafter a plea for help came from the Sixth's headquarters company in a ravine where it was being decimated by shells. Rushing there, Boone and his corpsmen found the only shelter a four-foot cemetery wall being chipped away by shell fragments. Working to aid the fallen men, they were spotted by a German plane that strafed them. The time had come to move to a better place. After transferring the wounded to a ravine, Boone returned to the cave, where he found so many mangled men under treatment that the stock of surgical instruments, dressings, splints, and other medical supplies was nearly depleted. In desperation and with the help of Lt. Col. Harry Lee, who had replaced Colonel Catlin, he found a motorcycle with sidecar that he drove alone over fields pock-marked with shell craters through a tremendous barrage of shells, past Vierzy to a supply dump. With the sidecar loaded with medical supplies, and still under intense fire, he headed back. Upon return he found a need for more and had to repeat the hair-raising trip.

Back in the cave the struggle to save lives continued, with need to amputate arms and legs and treat wounds under the crudest of conditions, along with the frustration of losing many lives. It was a bloody, grisly atmosphere, made worse when Boone's immediate superior, Farwell, suffered a nervous breakdown.

As evening approached, a way appeared to evacuate the wounded from the overcrowded cave. Packard trucks that brought ammunition to the front carried wounded to the rear.

The Soissons operation was an overwhelming success. For Boone's participation, he received the following citation:

The President of the United States in the name of The Congress takes pleasure in presenting the MEDAL OF HONOR to

LIEUTENANT JOEL T. BOONE
MEDICAL CORPS
UNITED STATES NAVY

for service as set forth in the following
CITATION:

For extraordinary heroism, conspicuous gallantry, and intrepidity while serving with the Sixth Regiment, United States Marines, in actual conflict with the enemy at and in the vicinity of Vierzy, France, 19 July 1918. With absolute disregard for personal safety, ever conscious and mindful of the suffering fallen, Surgeon Boone, leaving the shelter of a ravine, went forward onto the open field where there was no protection and, despite the extreme enemy fire of all calibers, through a heavy mist of gas, applied dressings and first aid to wounded Marines. This occurred southeast of Vierzy, near the cemetery, and on the road south from that town. When the dressings and supplies had been exhausted, he went through a heavy barrage of large-caliber shell, both high explosive and gas, to replenish these supplies, returning quickly with a side-car load, and administered them in saving the lives of the wounded. A second trip, under the same conditions and for the same purpose, was made by Surgeon Boone later that day.

—Woodrow Wilson

Following Soissons the regiment moved on to Marbach, battle-scarred from earlier fighting. It was here Boone learned he was a major. For years thereafter, whatever his rank, he was to be addressed as Major.

After Marbach it was St. Mihiel, a large action for Gen. John J. Pershing's troops, promising to be reminiscent of what had happened before, only more of it. The work this time was to push back a German salient that had thrust itself into French lines for many months. The Germans themselves were retreating when Pershing's men attacked, and the action was not what was expected, but there was enough of it to be impressive. Artillery bombarded along a thirty-mile front from midnight to 5:00 A.M., September 12, when the attack began, with men climbing over the parapets and charging into desolate open areas. Boone followed, with shoes and leggings soaked from wading in knee-deep mud. He established facilities for treatment and transportation, realizing that ambulances should push as far forward as possible. He lost no time cleaning wounds, hoping to avoid infection. By the end of the day the Sixth had reached the outskirts of Thiaucourt, where he set up in a schoolhouse and his men captured a German ambulance together with its motive power, two large white horses. Detaching a metal shield of the Imperial German Army from the ambulance, his men sent it to the surgeon general of the U.S. Navy.

The division's next battle was in the Champagne sector, between Somme-Py and Souain, the latter locality known as a place of the dead because the town had become a skeleton of its former self. Not until the last minute did Boone learn that this area had been assigned the brigade, and that Derby had been appointed division surgeon and Boone named his assistant.

The second day of the Champagne battle, October 3, was the hardest. During the twenty-four hours ending 8:00 A.M., October 4, twelve thousand casualties passed through the Souain stations. Many wounded came from Mont Blanc, from a station there in a dugout entered by a long stairway and ladders, offering protection from shelling but difficult for bringing in the wounded and then taking them out. There was constant concern that the enemy might enter the lines and toss grenades into the dugout.

The last assignment in the war was the Meuse-Argonne. Boone and Derby found the battle an enormous trial, for it turned into chaos. Pershing had a huge force, poured into an inverted triangle, the front slowly widening as the Americans moved forward, up between the Verdun front on the right and the heavily forested Ardennes on the left. Divisions seized what territory they could, with barely room for artillery, not to mention trucks and horse-drawn vehicles of every description. Soissons had been a scene of mild disorder compared with this.

Boone was in on the final attack at the Meuse, November 1, and again it was a deafening, seemingly relentless bombardment, opening at 4:00 A.M., across every ravine along a five-mile front. The guns produced an acrid smoke screen, and the infantry, including the Sixth Marines and the other brigade regiments, went over. But this time it was different, for the war was in its final days. There was intense fighting, accompanied by a stream of German prisoners pouring into the town of Sommerance, many carrying wounded friends, sometimes American wounded. German medical officers accompanied their men, setting up their own stations.

The Second Division made an astonishing advance of six miles on the first day of the fighting, far ahead of the Eightieth Division on its left. The corps commander, Maj. Gen. Charles P. Summerall, ordered the Second to hold and advance to the left of the Eightieth, which was part of another corps. As a result, the

Second came directly into the Eightieth's line of fire. The Second's commander, Brig. Gen. John A. Lejeune, was furious with Summerall, at one point refusing to accept his order of battle. Boone was a witness to the affair. (He and Derby were quartered in Lejeune's headquarters house.)

On November 4 the Second Division's two field hospitals were moved to a château at Landreville. During the following week, until the Armistice, hospital surgeons operated on 282 men.

For all the hundreds of thousands, indeed 2 million, Americans in France at the Armistice, that day was remembered for the rest of their lives. Boone and Derby with the divisional chaplain, Jason N. Pierce, drove from Fosse to Beaumont early in the morning, learned of the Armistice shortly to be declared, and, entering the church in Beaumont, which housed a dressing station, faced an unforgettable scene. The building's windows had been blown out, save for the side facing the sun, and it was filled with wounded covered with mud, pale, and haggard. They lay on the floor, some on the altar, where their wounds were dressed. Climbing into the gallery, Boone and Chaplain Pierce found a hand-pumped organ and recruited an organist and pumper. They stood on the balcony's rim and called out to the men below. Everyone who could stand rose, and those who could not, propped their heads with their arms. All joined in "America" as the sun broke through the clouds and shone through the stained-glass windows.

After the war Boone went through a series of experiences, most of them humdrum save for a welcome back home from Helen. In March 1919, he found himself shuffling papers at a desk in Washington in the navy's Bureau of Medicine and Surgery. Part of his duties consisted of a survey of Red Cross facilities, and it entailed a transcontinental train trip, which Joel and Helen made together, their first, though it was to be followed by many others. An amusing incident occurred on one such trip, many years later during World War II, when Boone in uniform bedecked with ribbons was handed a menu in the Santa Fe Chief diner bearing this hand-written note: "I am Pvt Red Skelton. All in fun. I am being dared to say, 'No good conduct ribbon?'"[11]

Receiving Croix de Guerre with palm from Assistant Secretary of the
Navy, Franklin D. Roosevelt

In the spring of 1920 there was a recurrence of the malaria contracted in Haiti. While at the bureau Boone received two Croix de Guerres, the second pinned on him by Assistant Secretary of the Navy Franklin D. Roosevelt, tall, handsome, vigorous. One night in January 1921, Boone found himself at the site of the disastrous collapse of the roof of the Knickerbocker Theater at Eighteenth Street and Columbia Road, a catastrophe caused by heavy snow. He teamed up with a fellow naval officer, Richard E. Byrd, helping bring out individuals trapped under piles of steel, concrete, plaster, and furniture. Boone and Byrd set up a station in a nearby church, reminiscent of experiences not long past.

As a recipient of the Medal of Honor, Boone was an honorary pallbearer at the interment of the unknown soldier on Armistice Day, 1921.

2

Introduction to the Hardings

Every officer in the armed services wonders about his next assignment, and such was the concern of Boone in 1922 when for reasons he never quite understood he found himself on the way to the White House. He supposed it was his winning of the Congressional Medal of Honor. It might have been his friendship with the head of the navy's Medical Corps, although that was difficult to gauge. The admiral liked Boone, he knew, but how far the liking went, in terms of an assignment, he could not calculate. The assignment that came early that year was nonetheless to lead to service in three presidential administrations, and his memories of the personalities he met, which were to include virtually all of official Washington, would last the rest of his life. It was, in a word, an unforgettable experience.

1

Helen Boone's aplomb made up for Joel's nervousness as the two of them set foot in the White House for the first time in March 1922. A formal note had invited them to tea with Mrs. Harding. As soon as they realized they were to be the First Lady's only guests, it became apparent this was more than a courtesy visit, one that had to relate to Joel's conversation with the surgeon general about a possible billet as medical officer aboard the presidential yacht *Mayflower*. President Harding had delegated Mrs. Harding to check out the Boones.

The First Lady did her best to put the couple at ease, but Joel was afraid that sweaty palms and halting speech would reveal his anxiety. So much seemed riding on the interview. His record with the Marines in Haiti in 1915–16 and during the world war in France had helped get him this far. However, it did not mean he possessed the social graces to mingle with the president and his wife and guests. Although the Boones both came from small towns in Pennsylvania and were not accustomed to such rarefied atmosphere, they passed inspection. Within weeks, orders came to report on May 1 to the commanding officer of the *Mayflower.*

Unknown to Boone at the time, there was another side to his assignment as medical officer of the presidential yacht. Service on the *Mayflower* counted as sea duty, for which Boone was due after three years ashore But it was not in direct support of the fighting navy such as duty on a destroyer or hospital ship would be. It was true that in the 1920s there were no large wars and few small ones, even in Central America and the Caribbean or in China, that might engage the U.S. Navy. Still, one never could tell. Something might come up. Then a superior officer might decide that Boone had been too far removed from the navy's primary purpose.

Boone's familiarity with his new ship was as slight as his knowledge of the entire navy only a few years earlier; only through happenstance had he learned from an uncle that there were physicians in the navy. The *Mayflower* was a 320-foot iron-hulled vessel built in Scotland in 1896 for the New York financier and yachtsman Ogden Goelet. At that time it was the last word in yachts. Two years later, following Goelet's death and after the battleship *Maine* had blown up in Havana Harbor, the government purchased the *Mayflower*, fitted it with guns, and used it in the blockade of Cuba. In 1902 the ship commenced its long service as a presidential yacht.

The *Mayflower* had been part of historic events. On its deck, while at anchor in Long Island Sound, Pres. Theodore Roosevelt greeted representatives of the czar of Russia and emperor of Japan on their way to New Hampshire to sign the peace treaty after the Russo-Japanese War of 1904–05. It was from the deck of the *Mayflower* that Roosevelt reviewed the United States fleet at the outset of its round-the-world cruise in 1907 and upon return fourteen months later, early in 1909.

USS *Mayflower* (PY1) under way, circa 1900 (Official U.S. Navy Photograph)

Presidents William H. Taft and Woodrow Wilson found the *Mayflower* a refuge from the oppressive summer heat and pressures of Washington. Taft, a large man who weighed three hundred pounds, left a legacy on board, a huge solid-marble bathtub manufactured especially for him. Wilson enjoyed the privacy of the *Mayflower*, especially after the death of his wife in 1914 and later when he sought to be alone with his new bride, the former Edith Bolling Galt.

Boone learned that he was responsible for the health of the *Mayflower*'s sizable crew of seven officers and 315 men. He was also expected to look after the president, his family, and guests whenever the president's physician, Brig. Gen. Charles E. Sawyer, was not on board. Sawyer had been the Hardings' family physician in Marion, Ohio, before they came to the White House; the new president had appointed him to the Army Medical Corps reserve.

Boone found President Harding down-to-earth, kind, and affable, willing to go out of his way to make him feel comfortable. He soon noted the president's fondness for cards and golf and watching baseball and football games. At lunch the president sometimes discussed baseball with the chewing gum king and owner of the Chicago Cubs, William Wrigley, an occasional guest.

Mrs. Harding took interest in politics and business. She had been a partner with her husband as editor and publisher of the *Marion Star*. Boone noticed that she never hesitated to express her views. She would at times take issue with the president, and when the discussion became heated he would scowl, shut his mouth tightly, and sometimes leave the room.

The president's wife had many superstitions. One time when she was ill and Boone was helping her move from a bed into a chair, he reached for a pair of white fur slippers and put them on the bed for her to use. The First Lady rose to a sitting position and, despite her weakness, scolded him: "Do not ever place slippers on a bed! You ought to know that is very bad luck."[1]

Mrs. Harding's interest in the *Mayflower* and its officers was so intense that when one officer was detached without her knowledge she sent for Secretary of the Navy Edwin Denby and

demanded an explanation. Because she involved the ship's officers in social activities at the White House, she felt she should be
consulted before any changes in the *Mayflower*'s officer complement. She objected when Capt. Ralston Holmes quite logically
proposed that Boone, as the *Mayflower*'s medical officer, should
stay with the ship when it left Washington for overhaul at the
Norfolk Navy Yard. Arguing that Boone was too familiar with
her history of kidney illness to be spared for more than a day, she
had her way.

As the ship's medical officer, Boone had collateral duties
planning stateroom assignments, seating at meals, and such
activities as movies and card playing. Now more than ever he
was forced to overcome natural shyness and develop social skills
that would prove invaluable in the years to come. In the course of
this work, he met many well-known people. Secretary of the
Treasury Andrew W. Mellon, one of the wealthiest men in the
country, made a lasting impression. He would come aboard with
less baggage than anyone else. His one piece was a briefcase into
which he stuffed a tuxedo, pajamas, and toilet articles. On his
stateroom dresser was an ivory-backed hairbrush with few bristles remaining, a symbol of the secretary's simplicity. Mellon was
such a shy person that upon meeting a stranger he would stand
speechless, then stammer before engaging in conversation.

Boone enjoyed mixing with the guests save one time when
Mrs. Harding asked him to join a party for bridge; he made one
mistake after another and was a disaster. Fortunately, there
were lighter moments and many a memorable occasion. When
HMS *Raleigh* of the Royal Navy berthed near the *Mayflower*,
officers of the latter entertained the *Raleigh*'s officers at a party
under a rented tent pitched on the dock. The *Raleigh* contributed
to the festivities by entertaining a steady stream of visitors in
pursuit of liquid sustenance forbidden on board U.S. ships. A hit
of the evening was the booth where a seaman dressed as a gypsy,
with earphones hidden under his turban, told fortunes. One
guest expressed amazement that the "gypsy" knew so many personal things about her. What she did not know was that up in the
radio shack her husband was talking into a microphone con-
nected to the gypsy's earphones.

Much about life aboard the *Mayflower* was formal. It was the rule for guests to dress for dinner, ladies in formal dresses, gentlemen in tuxedos. Serving as an officer called for an extensive wardrobe: frock coat, cutaway, tail coat, doeskin trousers, railroad trousers, together with blue-and-white service uniforms, cocked hat, epaulets, sword, medals, ribbons, and gray and white gloves. Officers and men paid homage to Mount Vernon whenever passing it in daylight hours. As the ship approached, they were called to quarters at the rail. The Marine guard appeared with rifles and presented arms, and the ship's complement stood at salute. The bell tolled, the band played "The Star-Spangled Banner," the bugler sounded "Taps," and the national colors were dipped. Visitors found the ritual a moving experience.

Not all aspects of life on the *Mayflower* were glamorous. Ventilation below decks was terrible, especially during a humid summer, with ports closed, only a few fans operating, and of course no air-conditioning. Conditions in compartments such as the laundry were almost unbearable. And mooring in the Anacostia River brought swarms of flies from a nearby dump. The flies blackened the underside of the canvas deck awning that provided shade for the president and guests. Boone knew food was being contaminated. To make matters worse, whenever the wind blew from the south it brought the smells of the dump. After many discussions with the District board of health, in which Boone invoked the name of the president, he succeeded in having the dump closed. Then there was need to refuel, a major undertaking, with barges coming along portside and dumping tons of coal on the main deck. The coal had to be hauled in hand-pulled dollies to the starboard side, where chutes dropped it into the bunkers. The all-day operation caused the ship to become filthy, and after each coaling it had to be washed and repainted. When the *Mayflower* converted to oil, life became much cleaner.

But it was the experience of getting acquainted with the Hardings that Boone found much more interesting than formalities and occasional trials such as the flies from the dump or the coaling of the ship. It was while on the *Mayflower* that Boone learned that one who makes rules can break them. It had been his practice to request of guests, upon arrival, that they refrain from tipping the mess attendants, explaining that recipients were subject to disciplinary action. At one point he learned that the president himself was tipping his valet. Boone asked Harding in a respectful tone to please discontinue the tipping. The president looked at him and said, "Why should you ask me to stop tipping if I wish to do so? And I do wish to do so."

"Mr. President, well, it was contrary to navy regulations."

"Who makes the navy regulations?"

"The Navy Department."

"Who approves the navy regulations?"

"The Commander-in-Chief."

"Who is that?"

"The President of the United States."

"Well then, Doctor, if I make the regulations, I have the privilege of breaking them, and I intend to continue the practice of tipping."[2]

Boone must have had this experience in mind when at Christmas he accepted from the president without hesitation an envelope containing a check along with a handwritten note. Harding took this opportunity to express both his and his wife's deep and enduring gratitude for Boone's attentiveness to Mrs. Harding during her illness and convalescence.[3]

It was, then, sort of a tip to the man who was against tipping.

Boone thus ended his first months with the president. He was unsure what it all meant, beyond the ceremony, which was clear enough. He liked the Hardings, and admired many of their guests, such as the millionaire Mellon. Proximity to the highest officials of government enabled Boone to see that they, too, had their purposes and concerns; there was profit to seeing that whatever one did there were problems and, the person involved hoped, solutions.

Boone had the feeling that all the panoply of power, the majesty of the presidential office, could vanish in a moment, almost in a puff of smoke, for there was a temporary aspect to living in the White House. It lasted perhaps four years, maybe with a second term, and then another occupant arrived. Too, the contrast between life in the White House and the modest Washington apartment that Boone shared with his wife and daughter, Suzanne, the latter little more than a tot, was remarkable. Every day as Boone boarded the *Mayflower* or visited the White House, he could see that whatever the regality of his surroundings, at the end of the day he returned to the apartment where he was only a small part of the hustle and bustle of the nation's capital. It was nought but life in an American city in the early 1920s, with the conveniences and the nuisances of togetherness with many people. One thing Boone could be sure of: it was a far cry from Pennsylvania.

2

Not long after Boone's assignment to the *Mayflower*, he found himself increasingly at the White House, caring for Mrs. Harding, whose kidney ailment flared up and caused much concern. She liked Boone, soon became attached to him, and insisted upon his presence even when General Sawyer, whom she had known for years in Marion, was available. This new White House duty presented two problems. First, Boone felt his attendance on Mrs. Harding might be disturbing to General Sawyer. Second, Boone found medical facilities at the White House to be primitive; a physician caring for occupants had to rely on whatever he carried in his medical bag. Sawyer had managed to acquire a linen closet on the south side of the long hallway on the second floor, equipping it with shelves, a folding table, and an overhead light. The transition from medical bag to closet marked progress, but some years were to pass before Boone, with support from a new president, installed adequate facilities at the White House.

Boone's involvement with Mrs. Harding began with the kidney problem that afflicted the president's wife in August and September 1922. She became ill on August 27 while on a *Mayflower* cruise—the last the Hardings were to make. Sawyer reviewed her extensive history of kidney problems with Boone, who consulted his seniors in the Navy Medical Corps, including

Rear Adm. Cary T. Grayson, who had been President Wilson's physician. Boone was flattered to have the general involve him in the case.

Mrs. Harding's condition rapidly deteriorated, and Boone found himself in the center of things. On September 7, the president came across Boone in the colonnade between the executive offices and the White House and said that Mrs. Harding would like to see him right away. Boone demurred, because he regarded her as Sawyer's patient; in absence of an invitation from Sawyer he did not feel it right to visit her. The president insisted on taking him upstairs to see his wife, who was in a great deal of pain.

Returning the next day, Boone discovered that Mrs. Harding was worse. He and Sawyer decided to discuss the situation on the telephone with Sawyer's physician son, Carl, in Marion, and Dr. Charles H. Mayo in Minnesota. Mayo promised to come to Washington. Upon his recommendation a call was made to Dr. John M. T. Finney of Baltimore, who came late that evening and, after studying Mrs. Harding's records and examining her, recommended an operation to relieve the infection he felt sure was in the kidneys, with likely involvement of the liver.

For several days it was a crisis situation. Unknown to Sawyer, the president asked Boone to stay at the White House the night of September 8 and Boone sat outside Mrs. Harding's bedroom between checks on her condition. At about 2:30 A.M. he was surprised to see the president, fully clothed, walk out of his study. The president told Boone he should be in bed since the illness would probably be a long one and require much attention. Boone followed Harding up the hall and into what he later learned was "the pink bedroom." The president looked it over and said, "This is much too large a room for you. Let's see if we can't find a smaller one." He led him into a small room with adjoining bath, in the northeast corner of the floor, saying, "I am sure this will be a more comfortable room for you and you won't rattle around so much." He pulled down the bedclothes, fluffed up the pillows, and said, "You're a little fellow. That pillow is too high for you. I'll go find one that will be lower for you." Scouting the closets, he came back with a pillow and then, concerned over Boone's lack of pajamas, said, "I'll go and get a pair of my own for you."[4] Harding was a large man, and Boone did not know how he would manage to fit into his pajamas. But when the president returned with a fine pair of blue-striped ones, he took care of that concern by rolling up both the sleeves and legs. Then, before saying good night, he went in to draw the doctor's bath and open the window.

Mrs. Harding did not improve the next day, and the physicians suspected she was going into a uremic, also septicemic, condition.

The following day, September 10, a virtual team of doctors held a three-hour conference. In addition to Sawyer and Boone, there were Carl Sawyer, Mayo, Finney, and Dr. George T. Harding II, the president's brother and a Columbus, Ohio, cardiologist. The issue was whether to operate that night. Each physician, in turn, argued the pros and cons.

That evening the president asked the team to join him in his study. The son of a physician, he had grown up in a medical atmosphere and was prepared to quiz the team, which he did extensively. He asked each physician to summarize his feelings and recommend how to proceed. Sawyer was against operating. He said Mrs. Harding would not survive because the shock would be too much for her nervous system. Carl Sawyer supported his father. Finney, the surgeon, recommended operating, and Mayo leaned in that direction. After hearing these opinions Harding talked with Mrs. Harding and returned to say she assented to an operation if necessary to save her life. Then, lifting his feet off the desk drawer, he turned to the end of the room and said, "Boone, you have not expressed yourself."

"Mr. President," Boone replied, "it is not becoming for me to voice an opinion. I am but a youth in medicine and sitting here at the feet of knowledge."

"There is no priority on knowledge in this room," was the response. "I want to hear from each and every one of you gentlemen, and that certainly includes you, Boone. You have been very close to Mrs. Harding's bedside. Now speak up."

Haltingly Boone said, "I have been almost hourly taking material for laboratory tests. Some I have conducted myself in a little laboratory I have set up in the northwest bedroom. I feel

41

the last blood counts and the urinalysis show some indication, however meager, that we could afford to wait a little longer before operating."

The president arose and strode off to his bedroom, saying with finality, "Gentlemen, thank you. We will not operate tonight."[5]

Boone feared he had made a terrible mistake by influencing the president to defer an operation favored by two well-known surgeons, Finney and Mayo. His fear was reinforced at 4:00 A.M. when Mayo, encountered in the hall, addressed him, saying, "Doctor, I could not sleep. I have doubts in my mind and feel we erred in not following Finney's leading suggestion that we operate forthwith. How did she seem when you last saw her?"

Boone replied sheepishly, "I have just recently left her room and I felt she has been losing ground throughout the night."

At Mayo's suggestion the two walked into Mrs. Harding's bedroom and stood at the foot of her bed. She was restless, seemed in pain, and stared at them strangely. She gripped her hands tightly, causing her fingernails to cut into both palms.

Carl Sawyer entered and after looking at Mrs. Harding said in a muffled voice, "Her last chapter is being written."

In just a short time a change came over the patient's countenance. She seemed to relax. Sure enough, the nurse discovered that Mrs. Harding needed the bedpan. Looking across the room, Dr. Mayo said, "Dr. Boone, we did not err last night. She has spontaneously relieved the obstruction."

Later Mrs. Harding told Boone, "I saw two indistinct figures standing at the foot of my bed. Now I know they were Dr. Mayo and you . . . I felt I was looking through the small end of opera glasses. When you were disappearing from my view, I knew that I was losing consciousness and I also knew that if I did lose consciousness, I would die. I was determined not to die and that is the reason I squeezed my hands so firmly that I cut the palms . . . until they bled."[6]

In later years Boone often thought of this experience as an example of how willpower can win, even in the face of odds.

After Mrs. Harding's illness Boone came to be treated as a member of the family. The First Lady showed her appreciation in several ways. She encouraged the Boones and their friends to use the White House tennis courts. She had flowers sent from the White House conservatory at least twice a week. She arranged for a car, chauffeur, and footman to take Helen and Suzanne for rides.

The president was as grateful and kind to the Boones as was his wife. The day before Christmas of 1922, Boone told President Harding that his father, Will, would be coming to spend Christmas and asked permission to be at home with his family that day rather than at the White House. "By all means," the president said, adding, "I want you to be sure to bring your father to the White House tomorrow morning. I want to meet him."

"Oh, Father comes from a very small town," was Boone's response. "He would be too embarrassed to come here to the White House."

"You tell him that I come from a small town and I am a very easy person to meet. I would like to have a chat with him."

When Boone returned on Christmas Day he found the president and Mrs. Harding, who was in a wheelchair, unwrapping presents with enthusiasm and laughter. Former Senator and Mrs. Harry New had joined them. The president looked up and said, "Boone, I thought you were going to bring your father to see me today."

"Yes, sir," Boone acknowledged. "He's down in the head usher's office."

"You go right down there and bring him up right up here immediately."

Boone carried out the president's instructions. Reappearing with his father in tow, he found that Mrs. Harding and Mrs. New had left the room and introduced Will Boone to the president and Senator New. Beaming as he shook hands, Harding opened a box of cigars. Boone's father was so nervous he mumbled in a barely audible voice, "No thank you, sir, no thank you."

Feeling he must inject himself into a social situation that was going nowhere, Boone said, "Mr. President, Father smokes cigars and smokes a lot of cigars. Much to my chagrin, he'll even break off an end of it and chew it."

"I love you for that, Mr. Boone," said the president as he threw his arms around Will and insisted that he take a cigar, which he did.[7]

Joel left the room for a few minutes to check on Mrs. Harding. Upon return he found the president, New, and his father sitting around the open fire talking furiously. It reminded him of three friends around a potbellied stove in a country store.

Gradually in the weeks before Christmas the president's wife had shown improvement, and by Christmas, despite the wheelchair, she was in fairly good condition. For this Boone and the president were grateful. But not long after Boone's father had visited at Christmastime the health of the president took a downturn and Boone soon became more worried about this development than he liked to recall.

The president's problem seemed to be the residue of a cold or what Boone suspected was influenza. He had a constant cough and tired easily. Sawyer and Boone implored him to rest, but Harding was a hardworking president, constantly in his office; he told the physicians that he had had little illness in his life and did not know how to give in to himself when he felt below par.

One might perhaps be allowed a speculation about whether the president's so-called influenza during the winter of 1922–23 was a sign of something more serious, in view of his death in San Francisco about six months later on August 2, 1923. It is worth noting that at the beginning of his presidency in 1921 Harding's systolic blood pressure was 180, a level that a later generation would recognize as cause for alarm. While it may have been even higher by 1923, records have not survived.[8]

But all of this lay in the future, and Sawyer and Boone could only deal with the medically accepted symptoms of their time. It was an era when cardiology was in its infancy, when what might have been signs of alarm in the present day would have seemed nothing at all then. Harding bore the appearance of a well man and was hearty in behavior—greeting people, grasping Boone's father when the two of them were speaking about cigars chewed or smoked, remaining up until the early hours of the morning working in his study, presiding over a group of half a dozen physicians seeking to ascertain the illness of his wife and its solution. He seemed all right. If Boone could have helped him in any way he would have done so, for by this time, after just a few months in the White House, he had come to like the Hardings very much indeed. They were ordinary people, to all appearances, and possessed none of the airs people of station sometimes display. The truth was, however, that he did not see any need to take extraordinary medical measures with the president, who as time would tell proved to be far more ill than his wife.

3

As President and Mrs. Harding became increasingly comfortable with Boone, they asked him to treat their closest political associate and friend, Attorney General Harry M. Daugherty, whose high blood pressure had caused him to suffer a cerebral hemorrhage. Daugherty had been the key figure in Harding's nomination and election as senator in 1914 and then in 1920 as president. An attorney, lobbyist, and politician, Daugherty was named attorney general by Harding out of gratitude for his support, despite press criticism that he possessed few credentials as either a lawyer or administrator. He proved a controversial figure in the administration. But then in most presidential administrations there are controversial figures, and Daugherty may not have been quite what he was said to be.

Daugherty, together with Boone, left Washington by train on March 5, 1923, with President and Mrs. Harding and their party, the entire group bound for a Florida vacation intended as a rest for both the president and First Lady. When Daugherty's health did not improve enough for him to join the presidential party on Edward McLean's houseboat at Ormond Beach for a trip down the Indian River, Daugherty, Boone, and a few others continued by train to Miami Beach.

In accompanying Daugherty, Boone unknowingly took on more than a medical case. Daugherty was receiving dozens of phone calls each week, and in the absence of a secretary Boone screened both them and visitors and acted in effect as the attorney general's press secretary. It was on this trip, incidentally, that Daugherty took it upon himself to announce that Harding would run for reelection in 1924—an announcement that did not have the president's blessing. It was an embarrassing thing for Daugherty to have done, for Harding was arranging a trip to Alaska that was bound to have some political overtones. In fact he was using the proposed trip by train to the West Coast as a survey of politics in those regions and had in mind also to set out in a series of important addresses what his program for the nation would be over the next years. All these things Daugherty had brought somewhat into disrepute by announcing Harding's availability, for it was not yet time to announce this sort of thing and all that Daugherty did was give the impression that the forthcoming trip was a political journey.

There was a puckish aspect to Daugherty, who was quick-witted and could say amusing things. The attorney general in a press interview told a story about one of his physical examinations at the hands of Boone. Daugherty claimed that Boone had asked him to stop breathing and left the room in response to a telephone call. He said he had written at once to Mrs. Harding and asked when that doctor of hers would return, or at least give him permission to resume breathing.

One aspect of the Florida trip that Boone found distasteful was living in close quarters with Jesse W. Smith, the Daughertys' longtime friend. Smith was heavy-set, with pink jowly cheeks, a black mustache, and huge brown eyes. Daugherty had befriended Smith when he was three years old, after his father died in the small town of Washington Court House. Smith played the role of grateful and loyal son, valet, nurse, and friend, and Daugherty came to depend upon the younger man, perhaps because his wife was a bedridden invalid who often was at the Johns Hopkins hospital in Baltimore and who spent winters in Florida. Smith idolized Daugherty, and any word of praise would cause him to purr happily. The two were nearly inseparable.

Upon arrival at the Flamingo Hotel in Miami Beach, Boone learned he was to share a room with Smith and was much distressed. He had found Smith loud, uncouth, impressed with his own importance, and forever putting his nose into someone else's business. Moreover, Smith was continually stirring up the ill

attorney general. To make matters worse, Daugherty asked Boone to care for Smith, who suffered from advanced diabetes and a slow-healing abdominal abscess resulting from a ruptured appendix. Boone did his best to help Smith, despite his feeling toward the man, but was frustrated by his patient's insistence on eating rich food and his total disregard for medical advice. It was a great relief when, on the return trip, Smith got off at Asheville, North Carolina.

During the trip and after returning to Washington, Boone noticed that Smith was beginning to get on Daugherty's nerves. The attorney general had been hearing complaints that Smith was behaving badly, speaking for Daugherty from an office at the Department of Justice even though he was not on the government payroll. Smith's duties were supposed to be confined to supervising the apartment at the Wardman Park Hotel that he shared with Daugherty. The latter became so annoyed that one evening Boone heard him tell Smith that if he did not stop throwing his weight around at the department he would have to move out of the apartment.[9] Shaken, Smith became less voluble, more withdrawn.

A change in Smith's personality was noticeable when, on May 29, Boone, Smith, Daugherty, and Daugherty's assistant William F. (Barney) Martin played nine holes of golf. Smith played an unusually poor game, having to be reminded when to drive, putt, and keep his eye on the ball. He seemed in a trance.

The next morning, Memorial Day, Boone was awakened at 6:30 by a telephone call from the manager of the Wardman Park urging him to come at once to Daugherty's apartment. Upon arrival he was greeted by Barney Martin. "There has been a terrible tragedy here," he said. "Jess Smith has shot himself."[10] Boone went with Martin to Smith's bedroom, where he saw a crumpled, doubled-up form on the far side of the bed nearest the window. Walking around the twin beds, he found Smith's body suspended over the side of the bed and his large head stuffed into a metal wastepaper basket. There was a hole in the right temple region surrounded by blackened skin and hair caused by powder burns. A bullet had traversed from the temple region above the ear in a diagonal direction, exiting higher up on the left side of the head. Blood had run from his nose and mouth onto his pajamas and the floor.

Martin told Boone how he and Smith had been alone the evening before, that Jess had behaved as strangely as on the golf course and Martin had been awakened by a gun shot. He found a .32-caliber pistol in Jess's right hand. On a piece of brown wrapping paper Jess had scribbled a will dated May 28.

After calling the District coroner, Dr. Ramsey Nebitt, Boone rushed to the White House, where Daugherty had spent the night. He ran upstairs, knocked on the president's bedroom door, and upon entering told him what had happened. Boone and Harding arranged to break the news gently to Daugherty. "Harry, Boone has some news for you, and it's very bad news," the president said. "So get hold of yourself."

Boone said, "General, Jess Smith has shot himself."

Daugherty blanched, his head dropped into his hands, and with elbows resting on his knees he leaned toward the floor. He raised his head and said repeatedly, "Why did he do it? My God, why did he do it?"[11]

The coroner made a statement with respect to Smith's death, and it was utterly clear as to what had happened. "There wasn't a single suspicious circumstance, and there was nothing for me to do but issue a certificate of suicide," he said.[12] Illness may have been one reason for the suicide. But there may have been other causes. No doubt Smith had been depressed at losing favor with his friend Daugherty. And, most important, he may have been fearful that a large bribe in which he had participated would be exposed. He had taken the bribe to facilitate a case before the Alien Property Custodian, Col. Thomas W. Miller, who later during the Coolidge administration went to jail. Smith took nearly three hundred thousand dollars and deposited part of it in a special account in the bank in Washington Court House owned by Daugherty's brother Mal. It was a saddening personal situation, in which Smith clearly had suffered a physical and intellectual breakdown. But it is important to add that Attorney General Daugherty was never found to have been involved in what happened. His error, if such it was, was to have trusted in Smith and in his probity.

Because of Smith's suicide and the later discovery of the bribery, people were inclined to believe that Smith had been murdered. There was no truth to such stories. Boone never had the slightest doubt that Smith's death was by suicide, nor did the Washington coroner. Smith's death has occasioned many speculations, most of them without any basis in proof. As for any involvement of Daugherty, that, too, is most unlikely. President Harding's connection with Smith's death was nonexistent, save for his friendship with Daugherty over the many years. Actually, the president had learned that Smith was misbehaving and asked Daugherty that he be sent back to Washington Court House, and this was the reason Daugherty was staying at the White House when Smith's suicide occurred—Smith was supposed to be cleaning his belongings out of the apartment.

Boone's association with the Hardings, Daugherty, Smith, and other members of the administration raises a question as to his knowledge of misdeeds on their part. He had little respect for Smith. In the case of the head of the Veterans' Bureau, Col. Charles R. Forbes, he had told the president that Forbes should be removed. Forbes, for whom Boone had refused to work three years earlier, was subsequently convicted of defrauding the government and sent to jail.

All Boone could say about the Harding administration at the end of his own long navy career, and when he had spent several years in retirement and could look back forty and more years, was that with the exception of Smith he had enjoyed his associations. Dougherty, indeed, had grown so close to the Boones that little Suzanne, at the age of three, addressed him as Uncle Harry. Boone never associated with Secretary of the Interior Albert B. Fall, who achieved notoriety through the Teapot Dome oil scandal as the first cabinet officer to go to jail. Thus, no Uncle Al.

3

With President Harding to the End

Early in June, 1923, soon after Jess Smith's death, Boone was handed a card signed by George B. Christian, Jr., Secretary to the President, and titled "Trip of the President to Alaska and Return." It identified Boone as a member of the president's party and asked that he be extended courtesy by anyone to whom the card might be presented.[1]

Boone was thrilled to learn that he was to accompany President Harding and party on a visit to the Territory of Alaska, scheduled to begin on June 20 with a 15-day transcontinental train trip to Tacoma and conclude in August with an eastbound voyage through the Panama Canal. This was to be the first visit of a president of the United States to Alaska since the territory was acquired from Russia in 1867; it also would represent the first formal presidential visit to Canada. Members of the party, in addition to President and Mrs. Harding, were the White House staff, three cabinet officers and wives, and twenty-two newspapermen. Along with Boone, the medical staff was to include General Sawyer and two navy nurses, Misses Ruth Powderly and Sue Dauser. Originally, the presidential yacht *Mayflower* was to cover the sea voyage from Tacoma to Alaska and return via the Panama Canal. But when the party was increased to eighty-five, too many for the *Mayflower*, the navy transport *Henderson* was substituted.

Boone was impressed by the planning, scheduling, and documentation required for a trip of three thousand miles by train, with stops along the way, followed by ten thousand miles at sea— almost half the distance around the world. Arrangements had to be made for scheduling train movements, station arrivals, reception committees, parades, speeches, seating plans at luncheons and dinners, baggage handling, and a myriad of other details

In those days before radio or television, the spoken word was the all-important means of communication. An innovation on the trip was installation of amplifiers on the observation platform at the rear of the president's car for use in speaking at stops. Communication between the train and the outside world was restricted to stops where a telephone could be plugged in or, alternatively, a telegram transmitted by wire.

Boone had to ensure that medical equipment and supplies would be on hand. With Mrs. Harding's kidney problems in mind, he arranged for a casket to be put aboard the *Henderson.*

On June 20, as the 2:00 P.M. scheduled departure of the presidential train approached, Helen and three year-old Suzanne accompanied Joel to Union Station. There they climbed to the observation platform of the president's car, where they were bid an affectionate farewell by not only Joel but also President and Mrs. Harding. Suzanne was a favorite of the Hardings, who at Christmas had bestowed upon her a large stuffed Airedale named Laddie Boy, a replica of the Hardings' live dog of that name. (Seventy-seven years later, showing the wear and tear imposed by a number of children and grandchildren, Suzanne's Laddie Boy is still a treasured family possession.)

As a roommate both on the train and on *Henderson*, Boone had the fortune to have the Speaker of the House of Representatives, Frederick Gillett, whom he found personable and informed.

As for other members of the party, Boone particularly enjoyed the newspaperman David Lawrence. As they were sitting in the diner one evening, Lawrence told Boone how, just after President Harding had made a speech appealing to the American people to respect the Eighteenth Amendment, he had asked Harding how after that he could ever take another drink. Lawrence reported that the president had looked at him and replied, "Dave, I prepared that speech with utmost care. I knew exactly what I was going to say and I wanted to say it. I spoke from conviction, and I can assure you that I shall never take another drink of liquor as long as I live."[2] During the remainder of the Alaska trip Boone never saw the president take a drink.

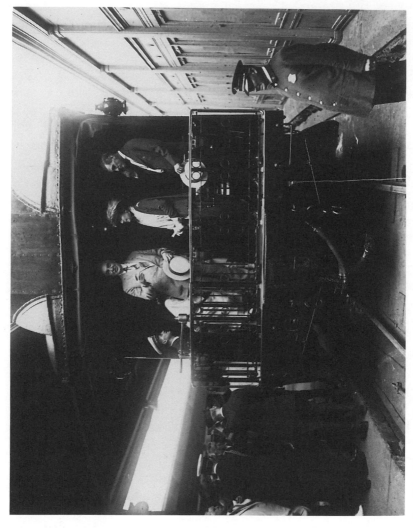

Leaving Washington, D.C., with President and Mrs. Harding en route to Alaska (National Photo)

Even as he lay ill in San Francisco, Harding resisted his physicians' insistence that he take a little alcohol and relented only as he reached death's door.

From the outset of the trip it is clear that Boone harbored concern about the president's ability to handle the schedule set out for him, especially in the summer heat and humidity of those pre-air-conditioning days. There were speeches, banquets, ceremonies at every overnight stop—St. Louis, Kansas City, Hutchinson, Denver, Cheyenne, Ogden, Salt Lake City, Boise, Butte, Pocatello, Idaho Falls, Spokane, Meacham (Oregon), and Portland. Then there were the stops that allowed local dignitaries to board the train for part of the trip, exhausting side trips to the future Zion National Park and to Yellowstone, arrival in Tacoma, and the voyage to Alaska and return.

For a president in perfect health the pace would have been trying. But Harding was not in perfect health, having suffered a severe cold, if not influenza, during the winter, and as Boone noted, influenza toxemia affects the musculature of the heart. The president had commented while in Florida that without a rest in both winter and summer he would not be able to survive. The schedule did provide golf as relaxation. In Kansas City there was a game following a two-hour parade. But the sun was so hot that the president's lips became swollen and he had to go to bed in advance of the speech that evening. The next morning in Hutchinson, Kansas, he revived sufficiently to drive a wheat binder through the fields, which to farm people gathered around made him seem like one of their own.

The transcontinental train trip and voyage to Alaska were eye-openers; never before had Boone seen such scenery or had opportunity to meet such interesting people. In Denver, Helen's brother Marshall Koch and family came aboard, to be greeted warmly by President and Mrs. Harding and photographed with them. The president had a knack for making people, young and old, feel at home. Salt Lake City made a strong impression, for in addition to the parade and speeches the party heard a program of organ and choral music in the Mormon Tabernacle. At the outset of the afternoon golf game Boone was amused by repartee between President Harding and Pres. Heber Grant, head of the church: each president insisted on deferring to the other as the first to tee off. It took the toss of a coin to resolve the impasse.

Under pressure from Sen. Reed Smoot, Harding assented to make a 285-mile side trip by rail from Salt Lake to Cedar City and from there by automobile to an undeveloped area proposed as a national park—Zion was to become its name. The train was the first one over a new railroad, which as Boone said "was a precarious and probably very unwise act."[3] Then a caravan of automobiles carried the party through canyons and passes over seventy-five miles of unpaved roads heavy with alkali dust that covered everyone from head to foot. To quote Boone, "It was an awful, awful motor trip," which the newspapermen hated.[4] Harding rode horseback up the rocky bed of the Virgin River. The president cut a figure in leather chaps, blue flowing neckerchief, and Panama hat. But he suffered from hemorrhoids, and with the saddle acting like a file, he could find relief from pain only by standing in the stirrups. When alone with Boone and Sawyer to receive treatment, Harding roundly cursed the ride. Boone had been told earlier by Sawyer that the president had a history of hemorrhoid trouble, that he had been advised to have an operation but had refused.

For Boone there were interesting experiences as the train continued westward: visiting the copper mine in Butte, observing Yellowstone, eating bear meat during the pageant at Meacham in celebration of the eightieth anniversary of opening the Oregon Trail. At Meacham, Harding held a powwow with Indian chiefs, relishing the peace pipe he smoked with them. Boone observed that the president enjoyed tobacco in any form and "had used it freely, I presume, most of his adult life."[5] He recalled how his own father and President Harding had smoked together on Christmas Day. While in Alaska the president would demonstrate his fondness for chewing tobacco when Boone made him a gift of Star Plug he had spotted in a country store. This was, of course, long before tobacco was recognized as a health hazard, but in view of subsequent events one cannot help but wonder whether habitual use of the substance might have contributed to Harding's death at the age of fifty-seven.

The stopover in Portland was to become memorable for

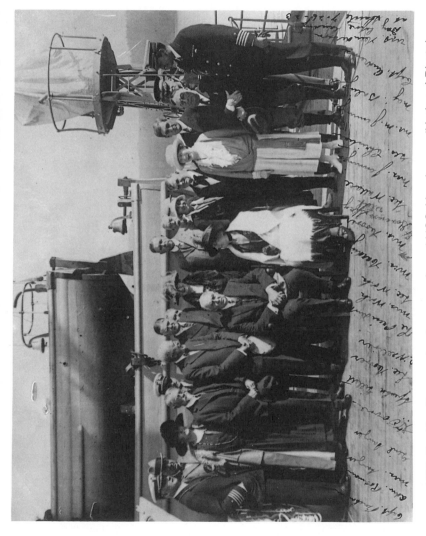

With the Hardings and entourage aboard USS *Henderson* (National Photo)

Boone: there for the first time he visited a veterans' hospital (No. 77). Years later as chief medical director of the Veterans Administration he would be responsible for managing all 172 hospitals in the VA system.

Upon arrival in Tacoma, Boone witnessed an earnest conversation between Harding and the man responsible for scheduling the president's activities on the trip, Walter Brown, destined to become postmaster general in the Hoover administration. Harding told Brown he could no longer stand such a schedule. "Unless it is radically modified . . . it will kill me . . . I just cannot keep up such a pace without dire consequences to me."[6] How prophetic those words!

As soon as this conversation ended, the president was at it, speaking in the stadium to a cheering crowd that had turned out to hear him despite rain.

As Boone boarded the *Henderson* on July 5, he could not help being reminded of his earlier voyage on that ship when in the autumn of 1917 he left from Philadelphia for St. Nazaire.

Three admirals came aboard the *Henderson* to pay their respects, flowers in bouquets and wreaths covered the decks, crowds cheered as the ship's lines were cast off, and once the ship reached deeper waters the battleship *Maryland* and cruiser *Seattle* fired twenty-one-gun salutes. Two destroyers accompanied the *Henderson*, one ahead, the other astern.

Boone and seventeen members of the party took meals in the main dining room, joined frequently by President and Mrs. Harding. For diversion there were shuffleboard, movies, and a band playing at all luncheons and dinners that encouraged singing and dancing. Mrs. Hoover, wife of the secretary of commerce and future president, asked Boone to teach her to dance.

On the inside passage the group was enchanted with the scenery—lush forests, mountain cliffs, snow-capped peaks, and later mammoth glaciers and icebergs. According to Boone the passing scene was so captivating that people would jump up from the dining room table to look through the windows or portholes.

The *Henderson* called at ten Alaskan ports, beginning with the Indian village of Metlakatla on Annette Island, ending on

July 22 with a call at Sitka, once Alaska's capital. There were two side trips by rail: from Seward through Anchorage to Fairbanks, with a view of Mount McKinley, and from Cordova along the Copper River to visit Child's Glacier, the single most spectacular sight of the trip.

But the purpose was not sightseeing but to improve understanding between the executive and legislative branches and the people of Alaska. Harding made speeches, met leaders, and received honors just as during the transcontinental trip. Secretary of Agriculture Henry C. Wallace and Secretary of the Interior Hubert Work met with local people to discuss fisheries, forests, mining, and agriculture.

The Alaskans had felt neglected and voiced criticism but now seemed consoled that they were finally getting attention. For their part, the visitors left with much better understanding of the territory. Noteworthy was concern for the environment and recognition of the need for conservation—some seventy-five years ago. Hoover deplored exploitation of the fisheries, recognizing need for federal intervention. Although he made no effort to upstage the president, Hoover was greeted wildly by crowds throughout Alaska, largely because of his well-known role as the one who had organized a program to feed starving Europeans following the world war. The trip to Alaska was remarkable when viewed from the later perspective at century's end. Imagine Pres. William J. Clinton taking a large staff and cabinet members and wives on a tour away from Washington for two months! Not only was Harding away for an extended period, but Vice President Coolidge was visiting in Plymouth, Vermont.

Boone's concern was the health of President and Mrs. Harding. When the train arrived in Fairbanks, Mrs. Harding suffered recurrence of her nephritis, and the plan for return to the seacoast by motoring over the Richardson Highway had to be canceled in favor of return by train. Boone was so worried about Mrs. Harding, far removed from medical facilities, that he wondered whether he would have to use the casket.

Apparently Harding found the schedule more to his liking than the transcontinental train trip. On the train from Anchorage to Fairbanks he rode in the locomotive and drove the engine;

at a place called Nenana he hammered a golden spike into a rail tie, marking completion of the Alaskan Railroad. Exhilaration in this fascinating land seemed to have a healing effect, or at least masked the fatigue Boone had seen earlier.

Harding, one should add, did not hesitate to tell one of his physicians if he didn't feel right. One day aboard the *Henderson* he showed Boone an infected finger that Sawyer had been treating. The president felt that the lesion needed to be excised but hesitated to ask Sawyer because the general's sight was poor. Boone fetched his medicine bag, sterilized an instrument, and was making an incision when he sensed Sawyer looking over his shoulder. Feeling a chill in the air, Boone dressed the finger and returned to his stateroom. Sawyer followed close behind, entered, and told Boone curtly he was never to go near the president or treat him for any reason without Sawyer's knowledge. Boone pointed out to the general that with all due respect, he was a medical officer in the regular navy, the president was his commander-in-chief, and any time the president sent for him he intended to respond without announcing an intention to do so to anyone. Over the next several days Boone continued to dress the finger.

But then as the *Henderson* brought the presidential party to Vancouver and the president took part in a strenuous day of ceremonies Boone's concern for the health of the chief executive became serious—matters, he sensed, were much worse than he had thought. Harding made an address to a crowd of forty thousand at Stanley Park, followed by a luncheon speech. In the middle of an afternoon golf game, as Boone played along in one of two foursomes, he spotted the president looking for a ball in the rough. Boone walked over and asked cheerily, "How are things going, Mr. President?" The response was, "Not at all well, Boone. I just can't get on my game today. I don't feel too well."

At the end of the game Boone sought out the president in the locker room. Quizzing brought forth only a repetition of vague symptoms and a comment that "maybe it's a gastrointestinal upset." When Boone said, "I am sure you are very tired," the president acknowledged it was true.[7] Boone advised Harding to go back to the hotel and get some rest, then looked up Sawyer and told him the president was not well.

Unease heightened that evening when Arthur "Major" Brooks, President Harding's valet and a man for whom Boone had much respect and affection, came to him and said that he and Sawyer "must hold the president down or he will break. He is hurrying too much."[8]

The *Henderson* sailed at 10:15 P.M. on an overnight passage to Seattle. Heavy fog was encountered and even though civilian pilots were on board and the destroyers continued to escort the ship, the lack of radar meant the *Hender*son's arrival in Seattle was delayed until the early afternoon of July 27.

When Boone saw Sawyer he was informed casually that Harding had been ill during the night with what Sawyer thought was an intestinal upset. Sawyer announced to the press that fish or crab poisoning had been the cause. Perplexed as to why Sawyer had not called him, Boone recalled the finger incident and suspected his colleague was making an effort to keep him as far away as possible.

What followed at Seattle proved to be greater cause for concern than what had happened in Vancouver.

At first everything seemed all right. As the fog was lifting on Puget Sound, Boone saw Harding accompanied by his wife come out on deck and ascend to the bridge for a review of the Pacific Fleet. The president looked tired. As Boone stood next to the arm-in-arm couple, he overhead Mrs. Harding say, "Oh, Warren, please cancel our going ashore. You are not physically up to it since you were sick last night." The president looked at the masses of people on rooftops, in windows, along roads, and on the docks and responded, "I would not disappoint that great outpouring of humanity, many of whom have traveled far and wide to come and see their president." He added emphatically, "Of course, we are going to go ashore!"[9]

Both Boone and Sawyer tried to persuade the president to heed his wife's plea, but his mind was made up. The party went ashore. Earlier the president's secretary had sent a message asking that the morning program be canceled, due to late arrival, with the afternoon schedule picked up at whatever time the party came ashore. The request was ignored, an attempt made to maintain the schedule in condensed form including a long parade, speeches, and even an Elks picnic for young people.

As Boone rode in the parade behind the president's open touring car and observed how Harding was doffing his straw hat, extending his right arm, and waving, he could not help but worry. Requests were being made for the president to stop here or there, and speak to a group or participate in some newly contrived ceremony, and he refused to say no. Through the afternoon and evening, whenever he had a chance, Boone asked the president how he was feeling. The response was, "I am tired. Of course, I am thrilled with this reception and I wouldn't want to have missed a moment of it."[10] It was apparent that he was becoming more fatigued with each passing hour.

At 4:30, when Harding delivered a long speech to thirty thousand people in the Seattle stadium on the subject of Alaska, Boone observed him closely. "He faltered reading his manuscript. Delivery did not have the punch...I thought that he would not be able to complete the address. Voice became more and more husky, seemed to have some labored breathing..."[11]

Another speech followed at 7:00 P.M. to the Seattle Press Club. As the former owner, publisher, and editor of the Marion *Daily Star*, the president was honored by the press club's publication of a fabricated "special edition" of the *Daily Star* dated July 27, 1923. The final words of an editorial in that paper were significant in view of subsequent events: "With the close of your visit among us, all too brief, we wish you Godspeed along your further journeyings, through all your arduous duties...and so to life's end."[12] Fate dictated that President Harding's life was to end just one week from that day.

The president made it to his train, standing in the station, ready to take him to California. Recalling how President Harding had bid farewell that evening to a crowd gathered around the observation platform, Boone had this to say: "I was standing immediately behind him...I can see him now...He took his straw hat. He threw it across the car and said, 'Doctor, I'll tell the world that one Warren Harding has had a most strenuous and fatiguing day and he is an exhausted man.'"[13]

Lying in his berth on board the train that left Seattle for California, Boone was unable to sleep. It was not the noise of the train as much as apprehension that there was something wrong with the president. He speculated that the president may have felt his health was at the breaking point. Fears were magnified the next morning when Sawyer told him Harding had been sick all night—the second night in a row—and would remain in bed all day. Boone pondered why again the general had not summoned him.

On July 28, Boone did visit the president several times but always in company with Sawyer and at the latter's request. He learned that the president had decided to cancel plans to visit Yosemite and that the train would now go directly to San Francisco. Mrs. Harding had stayed up all night with the president and refused to leave his side even as the second night on the train approached. At that point Boone and Sawyer decided to share their anxiety with regard to the health of both the president and his wife with the three cabinet officers on the train, Secretaries Work, Wallace, and Hoover, as well as Speaker Gillett; as a result, Boone was asked to stay at the president's bedside. Dr. Work had been a practicing physician in Colorado and president of the American Medical Association. All agreed that Mrs. Harding must go to bed the second night or she, too, would break. The only condition under which the president's wife consented was that Boone must remain with the president either in his stateroom or on a chair in the passageway outside the door. Boone promised not to take his eyes off her husband during the night. "As I sat there watching the president hour after hour," he later recalled, "he was quite restless and seemed very uncomfortable. I thought his breathing was quite heavy ... Not a soul was around except Brooks, the valet, took a peep in from time to time ... He kept inquiring whether he could do anything for me."[14]

To Boone's dismay, matters were much worse than they had appeared. "Sometime during the night the train stopped ... for the train to be inspected, possibly to get water ... Dead silence ... I felt very much alone ... aware of the great responsibility that was suddenly upon me ... I became instinctively conscious that there was more wrong with the president than we had foreseen."[15]

Soon after the train stopped, the president awoke and Boone decided this would be a good time to take his blood pressure, which had been known to rise on occasion, sometimes for an extended period. Whenever he knew that it was elevated, he would laugh it off, claiming that the harder he campaigned and the higher the pressure, the better he felt. He said there was a tendency for his family to have elevated pressure.

Boone did not like what he found in taking the president's pulse and coordinating it with his blood pressure. The latter was much lower than expected, lower than at any other time Boone had taken it. When the doctor opened the president's pajamas, had him lie on his back, and percussed his chest, he found the left border of the heart well to the left of its normal position. Sounds of his heart were muffled, with some irregularity. Boone deduced that the president had a dilated heart but was unable to continue the examination as the train began to move, picked up speed, and made considerable noise.

On the morning of July 29, Boone took Sawyer aside and told him what he had discovered during the night. After consultation with Work and others, a telegram went to officials in San Francisco advising that upon arrival the train would go to the freight yards rather than the station and an ambulance was to drive alongside the observation platform of the president's car.

When the president learned from Boone and Sawyer that he was to go off the train in a stretcher, in his pajamas, he scowled and withdrew into his stateroom. Unbeknownst to the physicians, he rang for Brooks, the valet, and reappeared in the sitting room, fully dressed, straw hat in hand. Boone and Sawyer remonstrated. The president said with finality, "Don't think for a minute that I am going to receive the governor of the sovereign state of California and the mayor of our host city, San Francisco, in pajamas . . . I will not be carried off this train!"[16]

Upon arrival in the yards, the president, pale and gray, greeted the governor, the mayor, and other officials when they came onto the observation platform. He walked off the train and into a limousine that took him and his wife to the Palace Hotel, where they were to occupy the suite used by both Presidents Roosevelt and Taft. The rest of the party, including Boone, Sawyer, and the army and navy aides, followed in other cars. When Boone saw the president walk through the lobby, into the elevator to go to the eighth floor, and then down long corridors to the presidential suite, he became apprehensive.

Just behind the president, Boone saw everything. "As he entered the living room and then the bedroom, still wearing his straw sailor hat...he threw his arms up in the air and fell across the bed with all his clothes on.... He was so completely exhausted that we made no attempt to undress him but let him lie there for some time before his valet...put on his pajamas."[17]

After Boone had put his things in the room directly across the hall from the president's bedroom, he and Sawyer prescribed medication, arranged laboratory tests, and, since neither was a registered physician in California, sought consultation with Dr. Ray Lyman Wilbur, internist and current president of the American Medical Association, and Dr. Charles W. Cooper, a San Francisco cardiologist. The medical team now consisted of five physicians, Doctors Sawyer, Wilbur, Cooper, Boone and Work, as well as nurses Powderly and Dauser.

Aware of the press's keen interest in following the president, the physicians released ten medical bulletins over the next several days, beginning with this one at 10:30 A.M. July 30:

> The president had a fairly comfortable night with several hours sleep. His temperature at 9 A.M. was 101, the digestive disturbance experienced on the boat is now localized in the gallbladder region. There are no peritoneal symptoms; the lungs are clear. The white blood cells number 10,800 with 82% polymorphonuclears. Kidneys are functioning satisfactorily and there are no disturbances of the nervous system, except those associated with fatigue. While his condition is acute, he has temporarily overstrained his cardiovascular system by carrying on his speaking engagements while ill. It will be necessary for him to have complete rest during the period of his acute symptoms.[18]

The second bulletin, issued at 5:10 P.M., July 30, mentioned "some cough and evidence of a congestion in one lung." It referred to the president's condition as "serious" rather than "acute," the condition mentioned in the earlier bulletin.[19]

Although Boone had been spending almost every waking hour with the president, he had slipped out of the room that day to summon Brooks and upon return was shocked to see that the president, despite admonitions by the physicians not to leave the bed, had gotten out and gone into the bathroom. Boone must have spoken to his patient harshly, for when Sawyer arrived the next morning the president commented that Boone had scolded him for getting out of bed. Boone took the position that while Harding was indeed the nation's chief executive and the young navy medical officer's commander, he was first of all a patient.

The care that the president received from Boone and Harding's appreciation of it was illustrated by an incident just after the president had been put back to bed on that first morning. Boone found it necessary to reduce manually the president's hemorrhoidal protrusion, much to the patient's embarrassment. The president said he was chagrined to have the doctor perform such a menial service, that he was "just a common citizen" and Boone was a "naval officer and government official." Boone tried to reassure him saying he was "merely a physician" performing the same service he would for any patient under similar circumstances.[20]

By evening of July 30 the physicians had become concerned over the president's condition and after a conference issued the third bulletin of the day, in which they said that "central patches of broncho-pneumonia have developed in the right lung . . . While his condition is grave, he is temperamentally well adapted to make a strong fight against the infection."[21]

The three bulletins on the following day, July 31, were more optimistic, noting "no extension of the pneumonic areas and the heart action is definitely improved," among other favorable signs.[22] Fifty correspondents were watching from offices set up down the hall from the presidential suite, and press coverage was extensive.

Reports the next day, August 1, were confusing, if not contradictory. As Boone later wrote, "My notes state that on August the first the president had a bad night last night," yet he acknowledged signing the 9:30 A.M. bulletin that the president was "fairly comfortable" and the 4:30 P.M. bulletin reporting "improvement in the lung condition." Boone stated privately, "The president was not doing as well as we would have liked the greater part of the first of August; he was quite restless." He went on to say, "We really felt a lift with the encouraging evidence that he was making some progress, even though slight at that time."[23]

The two bulletins of the final day of President Harding's life struck a positive note. The 9:30 A.M. bulletin remarked, "While recovery will inevitably take some little time, we are more confident than heretofore as to the outcome of his illness."[24] Following an afternoon conference the physicians issued their final bulletin at 4:30 P.M. stating that the president had "the most satisfactory day since his illness began."[25] While Boone signed these bulletins, he was the junior member of the team and never said to what extent his views differed. He did say Harding's condition was too precarious to discuss when the president might be able to leave San Francisco. Boone penciled a note on his copy of the final bulletin: "At this conference there was cautious optimism except on the part of General Sawyer who, we felt, was too optimistic that the president would recover."[26] In Boone's view, Sawyer allowed his long friendship to have undue influence on his opinion.

The president was feeling well enough that day to receive a visit from his sister Charity (Chat) Remsberg, who lived in Southern California. Boone was there when the president took her hand and said,"Believe I am out of the woods. If I had not turned the corner sometime yesterday, we would have just closed this chapter."[27]

Following release of the 4:30 P.M. bulletin, Boone went to his bedroom feeling that at last he could afford time to take a bath and change his uniform after a five-day vigil almost every hour of day and night. He had been willing to doze in a chair only when sure that a nurse, Brooks, or Sawyer was keeping an eye on the president.

That afternoon after a bath and nap, Boone returned to the president's bedroom to find Harding resting while Mrs. Harding read to him. Sawyer and the nurse were seated on either side of the bed. Boone joined and listened. Suddenly the president stiffened and a pale, frightened expression came over his face. He broke out in perspiration and became irritable. Sawyer reached over to take the pulse while Boone and Miss Powderly jumped up and went to his side. "I don't know what happened to me," Harding said. "A very sudden strange feeling that I have never experienced before."

As he started to move about in the bed, Boone implored him to remain still.

"But I'm so damn wet!" he exclaimed. At that, the nurse took a Turkish towel, dried him off and put on another pair of pajamas. After a little while the president said: "Florence, please go on with your reading . . . now I feel perfectly comfortable."[28]

Mrs. Harding continued, but not until after Boone and Sawyer noted the president's color and pulse were normal again.

At this point Boone said to Sawyer, "If you are going to be here, General, do you think it would be all right if I just went downstairs and stepped out in the street to get a little fresh air?"

"By all means, doctor," said Sawyer, "and get a little exercise if you can! It will do you good. I'm going to be right here."

So, I went on out . . . spoke to the newspapermen . . . kidded pleasantly to them, got on the elevator and went down to the first floor . . . As I passed near the cigar stand, I saw General Pershing looking over at the newspapers . . . I didn't stop to speak to him, although I knew him . . . I was afraid somebody might ask me exactly how the president had been in the afternoon. I did not wish to disclose this seizure that had occurred.

I went outside of the Palace Hotel onto Market Street, took a few steps . . . breathed deeply a number of times, came back . . . As I got out of the elevator . . . I heard somebody say excitedly, 'There is Dr. Boone, there's Dr. Boone."

I ran down the hall, increasing my speed the nearer I approached the president's room . . . As I entered the room, Mrs. Harding grabbed me hysterically, shook me by the shoulders, looked me in the eye with a very startled expression and said, "Dr. Boone, you can save him! You can save him! You can bring him back! Hurry, hurry, hurry!"

I saw there were a number of people in the room . . . Sawyer, Miss Powderly, Mr. Hoover and Dr. Work. Calmly as I possibly could, I stepped close to the president, looked down upon him, instinctively knew that life had been taken from him. To show that I was doing something . . . I raised the lids of the president's eyes, I touched both corneas with my fingers, then replaced the eyelids to the closed position. I stood erect, took Mrs. Harding in my arms. She looked stunned, as I said, shaking my head, "No one can save him, restore him to life. He is gone."

Mrs. Harding dropped her head on my shoulder . . . sobbed. Miss Powderly took her into her bedroom, gave her a sedative and put her to bed. Then there was a most terrible hush in the president's bedroom.[29]

As Boone regained his composure, he asked Sawyer what had happened. "You had just left but a very few minutes," was the answer, "when the president had a terrible seizure. He shook the bed violently, body quivered, his color left him . . . in what was a twinkling of an eye. The seizure departed just as fast as it came, and he had gone."[30]

Boone soon learned why the newspaperman had called out his name as he returned from the walk and got off the elevator on the hotel's eighth floor. It seems that the minute the president had been stricken Mrs. Harding had rushed out into the hallway and screamed, "Get Dr. Boone! Get Dr. Boone! Get Dr. Boone!"[31]

Devastated by the loss of this patient, the president of the United States, Boone could never forget what had happened. The experience left a permanent scar. He found it particularly hard to bear the burden of having let Mrs. Harding down after she had demonstrated such confidence in him. How he wished that he had the power to bring her husband back to life. But from what he learned, nobody could have saved President Harding's life.

When the physicians reviewed the case, it was agreed that the earlier spasm while Mrs. Harding was reading had resulted from a pinch-off of a cerebral vessel, while the fatal one was a large hemorrhage into the brain, probably from the same vessel. At midnight, August 2–3, a statement was issued over the signatures of the five physicians and its final paragraph read: "We all believe he died from apoplexy or a rupture of a blood vessel in the axis of the brain near the respiratory center. His death came after recovery from the acute illness was in progress. It might have occurred at any time. One of his sisters died suddenly in the same manner."[32] On August 3 a separate statement was issued by the two consulting physicians, Wilbur and Cooper, confirming and elaborating upon the midnight statement. Harding's death certificate, signed by Wilbur, stated the cause of death as "cerebral apoplexy following an acute gastrointestinal infection including cholecystitis and bronchopneumonia—instantaneous—contributory arteriosclerosis duration several years."[33]

The cause of death was to be a controversial subject for many years despite unequivocal statements made by the physicians who attended him—two presidents of the American Medical Association, two others with him day and night for months preceding his death, the fifth a cardiologist. It was perhaps unfortunate that no autopsy was performed, but Mrs. Harding did not want one. Harding was the first president in seventy-three years, since Zachary Taylor in 1850, to die from illness while in office.

Announcement by Sawyer that President Harding had suffered an intestinal upset as a result of fish or crab poisoning on the night of July 26–27, en route from Vancouver to Seattle on board the *Henderson*, proved a source of rumor as to the cause of his death. Even as the president lay on his death bed, Boone received a telegram from an old friend, George A. Sloane of New York City, secretary of the Copper and Brass Research Association, noting that newspapers were attributing the president's illness to copper poison resulting from eating crab that had probably become saturated with the copper frequently found in Alaskan waters. Sloane was concerned over the fear and anxiety that the report could create in the minds of millions of users of copper kitchen utensils. Boone penciled this note on the telegram: "Sawyer erred in making this announcement. It was not substantiated and later developments in president's illness discounted it." He sent the following response to Sloane: "Not General Sawyer's intention to convey impression that patient was suffering from cuprum poisoning. Boone."[34] But the food poisoning announcement became the source of tales that the president had been poisoned by his wife or in collusion with others or, alternatively, had committed suicide by poison. The result was *The Strange Death of President Harding*, a book by Gaston B. Means, who has been called "a confessed perjurer, a convicted criminal and a fantastic liar."[35]

A less serious charge was a widely circulated account that when Mrs. Albert B. Fall, wife of the former secretary of the interior, met President Harding in Kansas City on his way to Alaska she gave him the first news of the oil lease scandals that were to send her husband to jail, and the president found the news so demoralizing it led to his death. In 1939 Mrs. Fall wrote Boone from El Paso that she "never mentioned oil leases to Harding at any time" and asked for his opinion as to the cause of the president's death.[36] In response, Boone wrote the following letter:

1725 East Ocean Blvd.

Long Beach, Calif.

20 July 1939

Dear Mrs. Fall,

Your letter of July 11th reached me today. President Harding died of natural causes. There was no mystery to his death. No person nor any single incident was directly responsible. I feel he died a victim to the Presidential office.

Very sincerely,

J.T. Boone[37]

With the death of Sawyer on September 23, 1924, nearly fourteen months after the president's demise, Boone found himself the surviving White House physician from the Harding era. In this role he was to be pursued for the next forty years by scholars and writers seeking facts surrounding President Harding's death. As one professor wrote to him in 1960, "You are the only living person near enough to the event to give competent observation."[38] That same individual tried to obtain Boone's confirmation that the president died from acute coronary thrombosis rather than apoplexy. He quoted a letter from Dr. Samuel A. Levine of Boston stating that both Levine and Dr. Harvey Cushing, the noted brain surgeon at the Peter Bent Brigham Hospital, after reading the bulletins were convinced Harding had suffered an acute coronary thrombosis with mycardial infarction. Boone stood by the diagnosis of 1923. He stated that never in his years of practicing medicine had he been able to understand how anyone could presume to make a diagnosis at long range without knowing the patient's history or observing the illness firsthand.

The question of whether the president died of a stroke or of heart failure perhaps deserved more analysis than Boone was able to give it, if not at the time, then in later years, when heart problems became much better known, especially in the years after World War II. Cardiology was in its infancy in the early 1920s and had scarcely become a medical specialty. The first certified example of a heart attack appeared in Chicago in 1910. In that case the patient, who had eaten a heavy meal and gone to the theater, was then seized with violent convulsions and died within hours. The able physician who attended him, Dr. James B. Herrick, on impulse advised the pathologist to look for a clot near the patient's heart rather than to offer, as he might well have done, a general diagnosis of apoplexy, which was the word then commonly employed for what present-day physicians would describe as a stroke. Herrick published an epoch-making article in which he set out his findings, but the novelty of his diagnosis did not "catch on" and for years thereafter many physicians refused to believe in heart attacks.[39] Dr. Levine, whose letter to the scholar mentioned previously advanced the idea that Harding had died of myocardial infarction, was in long retrospect perhaps quite right. There was a telltale particular of the president's death that is characteristic of a heart attack: Harding died in a matter of seconds, whereas physicians now recognize that a stroke occurs at least ten minutes prior to death. But as mentioned, all of this was into the future, and Dr. Boone's extraordinary care of the patient, in the presence of four other physicians who saw things the way he did, ensured a diagnosis of apoplexy, or stroke.

On August 3, Boone left San Francisco, accompanying the president's body and the official party on a special train for Washington. Crowds gathered at every crossing to mourn the loss of their beloved president. As a thirty-three-year-old navy medical officer, Boone regarded President Harding as a fatherly old man even though he was not yet fifty-eight at the time of his death: "He never made me feel that I was but a young physician, showed me every courtesy, listened to what I had to say . . . He sought me out to treat him and to advise him professionally. He never questioned whether I was doing the right or the wrong thing."[40]

As the funeral train crossed the country, Boone kept an eye on Mrs. Harding, who remained in bed through much of the trip. He was appalled at the crowds that burst through police lines and caused the train to slow to a crawl as it passed through cities. Never had he seen such a display of public sympathy.

Met at Union Station in Washington by the new president, Calvin Coolidge, members of the cabinet, and Chief Justice Taft, the funeral party followed the caisson bearing the president's body and entered the East Room, where the casket was placed opposite the large windows between the portraits of George and Martha Washington. "To me it was a terrible, terrible stillness as we walked into the White House," Boone recalled, with the sadness that never left him.[41]

71

Accompanying mother and father of President Harding after the president's burial

4

First Experiences with the Coolidges

A White House announcement on August 25, 1923, stating that Brigadier General Sawyer and Lieutenant Commander Boone had been reappointed to the positions they had occupied during the Harding administration—Sawyer as White House physician, Boone as assistant physician and the *Mayflower*'s medical officer—may have been reassuring to Sawyer but did nothing to relieve Boone's concern over his relations with Sawyer.[1] He could not forget the dressing-down he had received on board the *Henderson* when he operated on President Harding's finger. All the while Sawyer had failed to share information on Harding's illness. Once Mrs. Harding returned to Marion, Sawyer began to visit there—whether to attend Mrs. Harding or oversee his sanitarium Boone did not know. In Sawyer's absence Boone felt responsible for President and Mrs. Coolidge. But whenever Sawyer returned to find Boone treating the president or his wife he again displayed resentment.

The need for obeisance to General Sawyer in carrying out White House medical duties was a source of frustration. Whenever the time came to conduct a physical examination of the president, the general invariably insisted it be brief. The younger physician recalled one instance when he was required to examine the president in the presence of Mrs. Coolidge and their sons, Calvin and John—hardly the proper atmosphere for examination of any patient, let alone the nation's chief executive. To make matters worse, when the president was asked by Boone to strip to the waist for an examination of the chest he merely unbuttoned the top of his shirt.

Boone vowed that in the future he would insist on making a

comprehensive examination in private regardless of the general's views on the subject. Having been involved in the illness and death of one president he wished to do everything in his power to avoid a repetition. In those days before "beepers," he made sure the White House's head usher knew where to reach him by telephone day or night—at dinner, the theater, or riding horseback on a park trail.

The wizened little reserve brigadier general, who had been granted his commission overnight at the behest of his friend Harding, could not hide his envy. Boone decided to broach the subject of his status to President Coolidge. The president attempted to reassure him by saying he had high regard for his professional fitness, he was a "White House fixture," and "Mrs. Coolidge would as soon lose one of her boys as you."[2]

Then, almost suddenly, things began to change, and so far as Boone was concerned the change was for the good. Boone tells of one occasion in which Sawyer seemed out of character: "He was unusually pleasant that evening and even complimentary to me. His attitude and manner were rather disarming and made me suspicious of hidden motives when he observed that he thought I would make good in private practice, saying I possessed the knowledge and personality and ability to be successful. I said to myself: why are you so pleasant at this time?"[3]

The general's enigmatic message soon became clear. Sawyer resigned on June 24, 1924. Subsequently, Maj. James F. Coupal, curator of the Army Medical Museum, was named to succeed him and Boone was asked by President Coolidge to continue at the White House as his "naval medical aide."

Boone could not help resenting that it was Coupal rather than he who had been appointed White House physician, especially after having served under Sawyer, whose most notable attribute lay not in professional qualification but in long and close association with Harding. A Boston physician who had treated the Coolidges during their vice presidential years, Coupal also possessed credentials that were unimpressive.

The navy's surgeon general, Adm. Edward R. Stitt, was apparently aware of Boone's feelings, for he had told him in the latter part of 1924 that he could be transferred from the

With President Coolidge and medical colleague, General Sawyer
(National Photo)

Mayflower and White House to a naval hospital if he desired. In the spring of 1925, Stitt offered Boone an even more attractive post—as senior medical officer at the American legation in Peking. Boone was ecstatic over this prospect. Yet nothing more was said or done about a change in duty during the remainder of 1925.

January 10, 1926, while on a *Mayflower* cruise, Boone decided the time was right to broach the subject to President Coolidge. After the usual predinner check of the president's pulse he asked the president whether they might have a little talk about a matter of concern to him. Coolidge nodded in assent, sat down in his comfortably upholstered chair, lighted a Corona, and listened attentively as Boone explained the navy's system of rotating officers between sea and shore duty and noted that by the end of April he would have been attached to the *Mayflower* four years, a much longer period than was normal for a naval officer.

Boone told of the opportunity in Peking, expressed appreciation for the many kindnesses extended him and his family by the president and First Lady, and pointed out that any other assignment would represent a step down from his present duty. He went on to say, however, that by staying too long in such a preferential position as was now his he would open himself to criticism from fellow officers.

After Boone had spoken his piece and a period of dead silence, the president removed the Corona from his mouth and responded by saying that he did not warm to people readily and hated to have changes made in the cast of characters working with him. He went on to say that he was grateful for Boone's attention to him and his family and that Mrs. Coolidge was fond of him. At the same time he acknowledged that he would be in the presidency for a limited period while Boone's career would be furthered by moving from one station to another over the years.

As dinnertime approached and the conversation neared an end, it appeared that the decision was to be left in Boone's hands. The president's final words, however, were, "Doctor, you go back over there to the Navy Department and ask those admirals whether they can conceive of any more important duty that a

With the Coolidges and entourage aboard the presidential yacht *Mayflower*

naval medical officer can perform than caring for the health of the president of the United States."[4]

Coolidge's reaction to the suggestion that Boone should seek a change of duty served only to confuse and bewilder, and on that same cruise he decided to discuss the matter with two guests, Frank Stearns, the Boston dry-goods store owner and the president's longtime confidant, and Governor Sproul of Pennsylvania. Stearns put it to Boone bluntly, "The president has put forward two propositions: one, he wants you, and two, will you sacrifice your naval career for remaining on duty with him?" Sproul, being a political animal, was less direct: "Doctor you are performing a great service here... We have our eyes on you. Some day we expect you to leave the navy and come back to your native Pennsylvania with us."[5] Years later Boone learned that Sproul had high hopes that he, the boy from St. Clair, might be elected governor of Pennsylvania.

Boone's mind was in turmoil; he suffered headaches and was chronically tired. He talked to Helen, Capt. Adolphus Andrews, who was his commanding officer on the *Mayflower*, and Admiral Stitt. Boone made two trips to Oyster Bay to discuss the issue with his friends Ethel and Dick Derby. The principal advice he received was that to keep his naval record clear he should put in an official request for change in duty to the Navy Department. On February 25, 1926, he made such a request through channels, stating: "It is believed that my best service interests will be respected if assigned to other sea duty or to a foreign shore station."[6]

Seven days after applying for transfer—that is on March 4— the Navy Department turned down Boone's request, signifying that the president's views on the issue had prevailed.

Meanwhile, during the transition in presidential physicians, Boone had turned his attention to caring for the president, and his wife and family—to the extent that the continuing presence of Dr. Sawyer allowed. This was not always the easiest task. Something of a hypochondriac, President Coolidge expected an attending physician to check his pulse every morning at precisely 8:00 and again in the evening at the stroke of 6:30. The president would always be waiting for Boone or Sawyer, usually seated in a high-back chair beside the marble fireplace. As soon as the doctor entered the room, he would pull up the left sleeve of his jacket and rest his elbow on the chair arm as a silent indicator that he was ready. He always expected to be told exactly what his pulse rate was. Whenever he questioned its accuracy, he would check by holding his pocket watch in one hand, grasping his throat by the thumb and middle finger of the other hand, and counting his own pulse.

It was necessary to be on time for this twice-daily ritual. "If I were ever late by even a moment or two... he would scarcely bid me the time of day... look rather expressionless and turn his face toward the clock on the mantel," Boone recounted.[7]

President Coolidge suffered from chronic nasal and bronchial trouble, and Boone treated him innumerable times, on occasion being called out in the middle of the night. The president was sensitive to pollens and whenever around horses suffered an asthmatic attack, accompanied by inflamed eyes, nasal discharge, an irritated throat, and shortness of breath. He used a nasal spray frequently. One time exudate accumulation in the crypts of the president's tonsils was so severe Boone had to clean the tonsillar areas several times a day, eventually eliminating the infection but never knowing what might have been absorbed into the bloodstream or what damage might have been done to the joints or other parts of the body. After Coolidge had left the White House and gone back to Massachusetts, he wrote Boone and asked for the "recipe" used to treat his nose.

Medical procedures by other physicians treating President Coolidge troubled Boone, especially administration of chlorine gas in May 1924 in an attempt to relieve the nasal condition. This treatment, still experimental, was highly controversial, and Boone did not think it appropriate for the president to be a guinea pig. Boone had tried the gas on himself and found it caused severe irritation of the nose and bronchi as well as dizziness. He insisted on laboratory examinations of the president's respiratory system before any further gas treatments.

The use of chlorine in treating a nasal condition reminded Boone of the work of a specialist who sought to control hemorrhaging in the nasal passages of Governor Hadley of Missouri.

On February 23, 1924, Boone was asked by President Coolidge to visit the governor at the Lafayette Hotel and try to help. Upon arrival Boone was shocked to see that the physician had packed the nose extensively, attached a piece of tape to the end of the pack, inserted the tape through Hadley's nose, and pulled it down behind the soft palate, finally tugging hard. The excruciating pain caused the governor to scream. The specialist was dismissed, and Boone stayed most of the night, eventually controlling the hemorrhage and alleviating the pain, although the so-called specialist had badly torn Hadley's nose.

Boone proclaimed that the governor would have been justified in suing the physician for malpractice, thereby illustrating his lifelong conviction that poor treatment of a patient is indefensible. He made no secret of his view that a physician's primary responsibility is to his patient, not his colleague. In choosing this as a theme of an address he was to make in later years to the august House of Delegates of the American Medical Association, he demonstrated that he was just as fearless in dealing with peers in the meeting room as in confronting the enemy on the battlefield.

The president liked medical attention of any sort, whenever he thought it necessary. One evening following a White House concert by Richard Crooks, Boone was called to treat Coolidge's throat. Finding a seat on the toilet, the president asked him to apply a corn plaster to one of his toes. As Boone, in evening full dress with epaulets and miniature medals, performed this menial therapy, he could not help but chortle to himself.

The very next evening, while at the theater with Helen, Boone was called in the middle of the second act to come to the White House at once. While his throat was being treated, the president asked all sorts of questions: "Where were you eating supper? Why are you all dressed up in a tuxedo?"[8] After asking who had accompanied him to the theater, he went on to say he was sorry Boone had to miss part of the play. Ever the dedicated physician, Boone told the president that taking care of him, Mrs. Coolidge, and their guests always took precedence over any social engagement.

Boone recognized the heavy demands placed on the president and First Lady, regarding them as "actor and actress on the public stage of the American scene." He tried to keep the Coolidges as healthy as possible, support them in their performance, and whether standing in the wings or on the stage, be a reassuring influence. He recognized a responsibility to care for his charges without disclosing to the public every detail of an indisposition and nonetheless keep the public informed. He deplored the actions of his medical brethren in cover-up of serious illnesses suffered by presidents before and after his White House service—especially the cases of Presidents Wilson, Franklin D. Roosevelt, and John F. Kennedy.

Boone's commitment to the patients under his charge was illustrated by his insistence that no one with a cold, flu, or other communicable disease should be permitted to come in contact with them. There were always people who were so thrilled to be invited to the White House or *Mayflower* that they would even get out of a sickbed to show up. Whenever getting wind of such a guest, Boone would intervene and insist that the person leave at once.

Coolidge had some habits that annoyed Boone. He was constantly nibbling fruit, nuts, or candies from the bowl on the center table in his bedroom, sometimes just before sitting down to a seven-course dinner. Although this did not seem to impair his appetite, it may well have been the source of his bouts of indigestion, especially after indulging in one of his favorite snacks, raw peanuts. At one point the president's indigestion and diet became such a source of concern to Boone that he not only worked with the *Mayflower*'s Filipino steward to revise the menu but also began to prescribe Elixir Lactopeptin. Coolidge liked the flavor, finding it gave him a lift, probably because Boone fortified the elixir with alcohol, thereby providing a small cocktail. When the president was under strain, he would ask for more than one dose.

The president had strange ideas about medication. Instead of taking two pills at bedtime as prescribed, he would insist on swallowing them before dinner, or he might double the prescribed dosage. He liked to invent his own "cures," such as a bizarre one for relieving seasickness, a malady that often afflicted him. Someone had told him that dropping cocaine in the external canal of his ear would reduce nausea. Boone went along with the treatment even though he doubted its efficacy. In June, 1927, when the president aboard the *Mayflower* reviewed the Atlantic fleet, a magnificent sight, he was too seasick to appreciate it. Apparently the cocaine Boone had inserted into the president's external auditory canal, as requested, failed to do the job.

Stearns once said to Boone, "The president has backwoods ideas on medicine, will only take medical advice when he sees fit to do so, and will rarely see fit to do so."[9]

Boone often spoke to Coolidge about the need for exercise, and the president did respond with early-morning walks in the area of Fourteenth and F Streets, checking out displays of women's clothing in the windows of Garfinckel's and other shops. This habit was consistent with his custom of accompanying Mrs. Coolidge whenever she bought a dress or hat, with the president showing preference for picture hats with red roses.

When an Amherst classmate, Mr. George T. Pratt, became concerned that Coolidge's walks did not provide adequate exercise, he made him a gift of a large mechanical horse. The animal came with bridle, bit, reins, and French flat leather saddle with stirrups and was stabled in the president's bedroom, so he could use it in privacy. The president enjoyed the horse and rarely missed a day, but Boone felt his routine faulty. Instead of following a conventional sequence—exercising, bathing and changing into clean clothes for dinner—he seemed to dress for the horse rather than people. He would take a bath, put on clean underclothes (with long sleeves and long drawers even in summer), starched shirt, black bow tie, and tuxedo trousers and jacket, and, finally, mount the horse and ride at a canter or trot. Controlling the speed of the horse by a lever in front of the saddle, he would ride until he worked up a real sweat. He would dismount, mop off his face, dry his hands, and go to dinner. Boone felt he was "putting the cart before the horse." He concluded that if Coolidge did not mind going to dinner in dress clothes damp with perspiration, why should he worry?

Such were the initial experiences with this so different president who followed Harding. Boone might well have thought that his White House medical service would be more droll than during the Harding era—a bit on the peculiar side but nonetheless interesting, albeit of minor medical importance. In this last respect he would have been mistaken, for not long after beginning treatment of the Coolidge family—which in addition to the president and his wife included John and his younger brother, Calvin, Jr.—Boone found himself facing tragedy in regard to Calvin, Jr.

On the afternoon of July 2, 1924, Boone went to the White House tennis court to play with John and Calvin and Jim Haley, the Secret Service man assigned to Mrs. Coolidge. Upon arrival he discovered John and Jim playing and was told that Calvin would not be playing that day because he was not feeling well. Boone went to the family quarters on the second floor and found Calvin, with his clothes on, lying on one of the twin beds placed in the Lincoln bedroom while the boys were home from school. Mrs. Coolidge was playing the piano as Boone asked Calvin what was wrong with him. Calvin said he was tired from too much tennis.

The afternoon that started out in such prosaic fashion was one Boone never would forget. "I felt his head," Boone recalled, "and found it was very hot, and I said that I would go to my medicine bag and get a thermometer to see whether he had any fever." Before he could do so, however, Mrs. Coolidge got up from the piano, went to her own bathroom across the hall, and returned with a thermometer. Upon taking the boy's temperature Boone found it to be 102 degrees. He observed:

> Calvin at fifteen was still a young boy although he had grown very rapidly and almost attained his full growth. He was a bit knock-kneed, which showed that he had grown too rapidly. He was a pale youngster, sandy hair like his father . . .
>
> I looked in his throat to see if there was any infection . . . It was negative. Then I thought there might be an inflamed appendix, so I proceeded to examine his abdomen. I could elicit no soreness . . . Perchance my hand, feeling along his groin, found some swollen glands. This gave me a shock and made me suspicious.
>
> I asked Calvin if he had bumped his shin. He was always a laconic boy and he said, "Nope." I asked him if he had any blisters any place, on his feet. He said, "Yup." I asked him where. He said,

"On a toe." I asked him how he acquired it. Well, he said he was in a hurry when he went to play tennis on Monday with us and he failed to put on his socks and he had rubbed a blister, he thought. I found a blister, almost the size of my thumbnail, on the third toe just behind the second joint on the anterior surface, a darker blister than one would ordinarily see, adding further to my suspicions and concern. I then looked over his legs and found some red streaks. Then I knew we were in trouble. I told Calvin to undress and get into bed.[10]

Boone called Coupal, informed him of his findings, and pointed out that they were not dealing with some simple illness. After Coupal arrived at the White House, the physicians took a culture for the Naval Medical School laboratory and prescribed various therapeutic measures for Calvin. Then they disclosed their apprehension to President and Mrs. Coolidge.

The next morning, July 3, Boone and Coupal met early at the White House, where they found that Calvin had had a restless night and was more ill, with a higher temperature than on the evening before. Feeling a need for consultation, they asked Col. William Keller, chief of surgery at Walter Reed Army Hospital, to confer with them. Upon his examination of Calvin, he confirmed some of Boone's findings but was also suspicious of appendicitis.

At this point Boone acknowledged "we were well aware that we were in trouble and that Calvin's illness would have to be announced to the press." Noting that all three physicians were members of the medical service of the armed forces, he recognized that it would be wise to seek civilian consultation. "We decided to telephone Dr. John B. Deaver, Professor of Surgery at the German Hospital in Philadelphia," who came down on the first train.[11] Again, findings were confirmed. Deaver, too, was suspicious of appendicitis but not sufficiently sure of it to recommend an immediate operation. He had to return to Philadelphia, where he was scheduled to operate all the next morning, but asked to be informed how Calvin was progressing.

On the third day, July 4 (the president's birthday), Calvin was losing ground, having had another restless night and even higher temperature. Boone and Coupal talked to Deaver, who said he could not come back to Washington until the following day and asked if he could bring a pathologist from the University of Pennsylvania, a Dr. Kolmar. The two were delighted to have any assistance.

A culture report from the laboratory revealed staphylococcus aureus. "We were relieved it was not a streptococcus, because in those days we had more dread of a streptococcus than we had of a staphylococcus," Boone said.[12] Blood counts and smears were showing heavier infection. Leukocyte or white cells did not go above normal, which was a concern. Calvin was not marshaling the defensive forces produced by his own body. Boone remained at the White House night and day.

July 5, Deaver returned from Philadelphia, bringing Kolmar for laboratory work. Deaver decided Calvin should be moved to a hospital, and since Dr. Keller at Walter Reed was already on the case, Calvin was transferred by ambulance. Laboratory tests as well as examination of excreta showed growth of staphylococcus aureus. Assisted by Keller, Deaver decided to make an incision over the left tibia and chisel some of the bone for cultures to determine if the infection had traveled. When the results were available two days later, the physicians had proof that Calvin had a generalized staphylococcus aureo septicemia, or blood poisoning.

July 6, after a very bad night, the patient was going from bad to worse. Calvin's blood type was announced in the newspapers in an effort to find blood for transfusions. The president and Mrs. Coolidge stayed at Walter Reed in a room across the hall. Concluding there was nothing more he could do, Deaver returned to Philadelphia. Kolmar stayed on as consultant in pathology. Boone and Coupal never left the hospital.

Respiratory symptoms appeared, and oxygen had to be administered. July 7, while Boone was preparing to administer oxygen, a long valve on the tanks accidentally opened, causing the heavy metal head of the container to explode, striking Boone over the cardiac region, stunning him. His pulse was affected, and he became nauseated. In the midst of Calvin's crisis Boone was put to bed across the hall, but as soon as he was able he returned to Calvin's room, realizing the boy's condition was desperate.

It was an appalling scene, that day long ago, July 7, 1924. President Coolidge was in the sickroom for hours at a time. Calvin lapsed into unconsciousness for lengthening periods. At one point Boone heard him say, "I surrender." Leaning over him and speaking as one who had experienced much combat, the doctor responded, "No, Calvin, never surrender!"[13]

The president could not believe his son was on the verge of death. He stood there with great dignity, almost immobile, never showing emotion but obviously tense within while gazing at his son. He reached into his pocket and pulled out a gold locket, which Boone learned later contained a lock of his mother's hair that was almost identical in texture and color to Calvin's sandy-reddish hair.

The President pressed the locket into the hand of Calvin, who, at first, was conscious enough to grasp it but dropped it to the floor as he dozed off. Repeating this process, the president had to hold the locket in Calvin's hand, tightly closed, because the boy had drifted into unconsciousness from which he never recovered. As the president used one of his hands to hold his son's hand with the locket enclosed in it, he used the other to caress Calvin's forehead and brush back his glossy hair. It was a heart-rending scene.

One of the final diagnostic evidences was the terminal one, an ileus or intestinal obstruction. The youth was overwhelmed with infection, and with the ileus his heart began to falter, until his pulse ceased. No therapeutic measure then known to medical science was able to save this boy's life.

When it was known on July 7 that the battle was lost, Mrs. Coolidge entered the room and, standing alongside the president, gazed silently at her son in death. The two quietly left the death chamber, expressed their thanks to all who had attended Calvin, and returned to the White House. Boone and others marveled at their fortitude and self-control, evident through the vigil.

Boone had this to say:

> In . . . less than a year it had been my tragic experience to stand at the bedside of two of my patients who expired. Terribly, terribly shocking . . . one I do not believe I have ever recovered from . . . As

86

Mrs. Boone heard the reports . . . at Walter Reed, she drove out to the hospital and sat waiting for hours until I would come out to join her. I had been standing a vigil, laboring almost incessantly five nights and five days, very little break. As I rode home with my wife it was in silence. I was too stunned and too sorrowful to speak . . . physically and mentally drained of strength.[14]

The nation was stunned by this tragedy. Sorrow must be felt for the parents of any youth taken on the threshold of manhood, but as Boone observed, "When the victim was the son of the President of the United States and his wonderful wife, the nation wrapped itself in deep mourning. Each citizen seemed to have been brought closer and closer to the head of the nation and its First Lady."[15]

Calvin's body lay in the East Room, followed by services there, as well as in Northampton and Plymouth. Helen and Joel were present.

The president later wrote to a friend, who had also lost a young son, that their sons ". . . by the grace of God, have the privilege of being boys throughout Eternity."[16]

To Boone, Calvin's death represented not only the loss of a precious human life but also the loss of a dear friend, one with whom he had enjoyed many moments of play and banter. He especially appreciated Calvin's keen sense of humor, illustrated in his telling of an evening at the White House in March 1924, just four months before Calvin's death: "Mrs. Coolidge, Calvin, Dr. Irvine, who was headmaster of Mercersburg Academy, and I were just ending a game of pool. Dr. Irvine, having scored the fewest points in the game, caused this Mercersburg student to remark, 'Well, Doctor, you give splendid evidence of not having wasted your youth.'"[17]

5

The Golden Twenties in the White House

Despite the era's reputation, the 1920s in the White House were a modest, careful time, made more so by a modest, frugal president—Calvin Coolidge. For the Boone family they were not the golden era so often written about. Joel Boone's lieutenant commander's pay in the peacetime navy was low, making it difficult to experience the entertainment, recreation, and other extras of life enjoyed by many. Being part of the capital's official life had its glamorous side, but the extra expense was hard on the family budget and his time was not his own.

Boone's first contact with the Coolidges had taken place a year or so before they moved into the White House. Having heard that he was an alumnus of Mercersburg Academy, Mrs. Coolidge had invited him to tea in the Willard Hotel suite then occupied by the vice president and his family to talk about a preparatory school for her sons. She explained that since both she and the vice president were New Englanders, they would ordinarily prefer that the boys attend a school in New England. Living in Washington, however, they would like to have them in a school closer at hand.

It was the beginning of a long friendship. One of the high points in Boone's life was the opportunity to show Mercersburg to Grace Coolidge, leading to John and Calvin's enrollment there and a lifelong association with John and his mother. Boone was successful in transmitting to both mother and son his boundless enthusiasm for Mercersburg, and each of them was eventually to serve as a trustee of the academy.

After the Coolidges moved into the White House, Boone found himself spending time with John and Calvin, Jr., when they were home from school. They rode horseback, played tennis, shot pool, went sightseeing in Washington, and had lunch aboard the *Mayflower*. One time Boone was boxing with John in the living quarters when the president appeared. With a frown, the nation's chief executive said pointedly, "You are almost as young as John, but not quite."[1] Boone concluded that he disapproved of the boxing but did not let the comment bother him.

The boys asked Boone to help them select suits and hats from among the things brought home from the haberdasher's shop that they visited with Brooks, the president's valet. But here the president's desires proved paramount. Boone was with them one day when the president arrived from the executive offices, asked John and Calvin to try on the suits, and without asking the boys their preferences simply pointed his finger and said in his nasal twang, "You will take that one, John. Calvin, you will take that one."[2] After going through the same process with the hats, the president abruptly left the room.

President Coolidge had such a tight rein on his boys' behavior that he even dictated when they should wear overshoes and ordered that they should wear suspenders, not just belts, to hold up their trousers. The president continued to select John's clothes even during his college years. Both boys were required to wear tuxedoes at dinner, served regularly in the large state dining room rather than in the private dining room—out of respect for the office of president, according to Boone.

The doctor's connection with the boys was close. He found them both attractive, and the Mercersburg tie was a factor. Calvin, Jr.'s death made the bond of the academy permanent; it was almost difficult to discuss, it was so close. In 1926 in the autumn, a glorious season in Pennsylvania and so reminiscent of rural Vermont, the academy dedicated its beautiful new chapel. Coolidge as vice president had broken its ground. Mrs. Coolidge attended the dedication in the company of Helen and Joel, along with representatives of fifty-five schools, including colleges and universities across the United States—from Harvard in the East to Stanford in the West. Boone remembered sitting in silence during the dedication in what is widely regarded as one of the finest Gothic structures in the land, with the organ and carillon playing. He was sure Mrs. Coolidge's thoughts were concentrated on her son Calvin as her eyes focused on the chancel's glistening gold cross that she and her husband had given in Calvin's memory. At the conclusion of the ceremony the president's senior army aide, Colonel Cheney, commented that now that he had experienced the spirit of Mercersburg he knew the source of Boone's successes. Boone denied any successes in his life but said that the colonel had put his finger on the source of the doctor's inspiration.

Mrs. Coolidge was so moved by the experience as to say that she would have been willing to give up five years of her life for the sake of being there.

Duty as medical officer on board the *Mayflower*, in addition to being assistant physician at the White House, offered a double opportunity to become acquainted with Mrs. Coolidge. When the president and wife took their first Potomac River cruise on September 15, 1923, they made clear that Boone was to be treated as a member of the official family by inviting him to tea and dinner on board.

It was on this cruise that Mrs. Coolidge invited Boone to bring Suzanne, aged three and one-half, to the White House. Boone did so the very next day, initiating an enduring relationship between Mrs. Coolidge and his daughter. According to Suzanne, Mrs. Coolidge, known for her radiant smile and twinkling eyes, was everything the president was not—animated, affectionate, sociable. Within two months, Mrs. Coolidge had become so fond of little Suzanne that she asked her to stay overnight at the White House while Helen and Joel made a trip to Mercersburg.

For Suzanne the night of November 14, 1923, was a memorable occasion, which Mrs. Coolidge was to record in a touching little essay, "Suzanne Spends a Night at the White House."[3] (see appendix). The youngster would never forget sleeping in the nine-foot-long Lincoln bed that had been occupied not only by Pres. Abraham Lincoln but also by President Wilson when he was recovering from his stroke. Years later one of Suzanne's small children was to boast to a friend, "My mother slept with Abraham Lincoln."[4]

The Boones returned from their overnight trip to learn that their daughter had eaten breakfast with President and Mrs. Coolidge on a card table in the president's bedroom. According to Mrs. Coolidge, during breakfast Suzanne looked at her husband intently and asked, "Do you love me, Mr. President?" He replied with more feeling than usual, "I certainly do love you, Suzanne."[5]

The president did, in fact, take quite a shine to Suzanne and showed his affection by offering her chewing gum each time they met—usually a package but on one occasion an entire box. Suzanne learned that he had shared a full case that had been a gift from the gum magnate, William Wrigley.

When Suzanne accompanied her father to the White House the president would ask that she be brought into his bedroom as he shaved. Once as she was being carried into the bedroom by Mrs. Coolidge, she was scratched on the legs by the Coolidges' collie, Rob Roy. The president scowled and remarked that Suzanne should have been wearing long stockings.

As the ties between the Coolidges and Boones grew stronger, Mrs. Coolidge made a point of sending boxes of flowers from the White House gardens or hothouses to the Boone apartment as tokens of her affection for the physician and his little family.

For the Boones, a highlight of the spring of 1926 was the Ringling Brothers and Barnum & Bailey Circus, which they attended on May 1 as guests of President and Mrs. Coolidge. With the by-then-six-year-old Suzanne on Mrs. Coolidge's lap and John Ringling seated alongside, photographers caught President Coolidge in a rare smile, a scene reproduced in newspapers throughout the country.

Without asking Mrs. Coolidge where she would like to spend the summer, the president in 1926 decided they would go to the Adirondacks. The decision was met with little enthusiasm among the White House staff, who felt the president would be restless in that isolated area and get on people's nerves. From the start, the president turned out to be irritable. Helen accompanied Joel on a drive to the Adirondacks, where he was to be with the party for the summer, but because of the expense she had to return to Washington after only one day in the mountains. The Coolidges occupied White Pine Camp, fourteen buildings

John Ringling, President and Mrs. Coolidge, and Suzanne Boone
at the circus (Courtesy of AP/Wide World Photos)

scattered through the woods near Saranac Lake and Paul Smith's Hotel. Boone pitched his tent near the edge of the lake where he had a beautiful view, except when it rained, which it did often. Next to his tent were others, set up for a dispensary and for billeting the marine guard.

Fishing was the president's diversion that summer, and Osgood Pond seemed to have been reserved for his private use. One day in mid-July, when he came in to show Mrs. Coolidge the good catch that he had made, she asked to see his hands. She asked how he was able to keep them so clean when he had to take fish off the hook. Sheepishly he acknowledged that Secret Service men not only took the fish off the hooks but also baited them. She learned, much to her disgust, that he wore gloves when he fished.

The president and First Lady led a dull life that summer, remaining in isolation and doing little entertaining. Coolidge would go into the office at 10:00 A.M., and on most days finish his work in an hour.

With few outsiders, Boone had opportunity to observe the family firsthand. It was not a happy summer. Boone became painfully aware of this when the Secret Service man assigned to Mrs. Coolidge, Jim Haley, complained to him about the president's attitude toward his wife, saying he did not give her enough consideration or attention. Apparently Haley attempted to make up for this by showering Mrs. Coolidge with attention, for they were often seen walking, talking, and laughing together. Little did Boone realize that the relationship would become a cause célèbre the next year when during the presidential vacation in the Black Hills of South Dakota Haley failed to return when expected from a walking trip with Mrs. Coolidge; the president sent Haley back to Washington.

The newspapermen at the Adirondack camp began commenting that President and Mrs. Coolidge seemed unhappy and speculated as to the cause. Boone felt that Mrs. Coolidge looked unwell and lacked her usual high spirits and interest in things. Loquaciousness had been supplanted by silences and brooding. As her physician, Boone was concerned, and he soon had the opportunity to query Mr. and Mrs. Stearns. They seemed to think the problem was disagreement between the president and his wife as to how to deal with their son John. The president was inclined to be severe, whereas Mrs. Coolidge was sympathetic and loving. Both the Stearnses and Boone felt John was "farmed out" too much in military camp or college, missing the influence of his mother in development of work habits and social interests. It hurt Boone to see John going through such a difficult period and he tried to spend as much time as possible with him. In telling his mother of one of their outings in Saranac, John's eyes lit up as he said, "It was the berries!"[6] The age difference of seventeen years made the relation akin to that of an older and younger brother. When asked about this seventy years later, John said, "Joel was somebody special." He added enthusiastically, "You know he's the one who introduced us to Mercersburg."[7]

The day after his talk with the Stearnses, Boone approached Mrs. Coolidge when she came in from canoeing. She said quite frankly that she and the president were not at all in accord over John's upbringing, that the president did not understand him and made no attempt to do so. John was reprimanded so constantly he did not like to be at home. Boone recalled John's comment the previous summer when he had come from Camp Devens, the civilian military training camp in Massachusetts, to White Court, the summer White House in Swampscott. Not permitted to play tennis, he said that he "might as well be in the penitentiary as White Court."[8]

Mrs. Coolidge went on to say that the president had been too absorbed in his work to understand his boys as they grew up. When she had asked him whether he intended to go to Mercersburg for the chapel dedication, he replied that he would be a fine one to stand up and speak to the boys when he could not even handle his own son. In Massachusetts, Coolidge had seen the boys only the one day a week he was home from Boston and usually had been tired and irritable. He did not want John to go to parties and did not like some of the youth's companions, although he was fond of John's sweetheart and future bride, Florence Trumbull.

Mrs. Coolidge said the president had determined that if John did not do well in college he would make him go to work to

At Mercersburg Academy with Mrs. Coolidge, Suzanne, and Helen
for unveiling of portrait

earn his living. She assured Boone she would always stand by John, no matter what. She wrote to him daily. At the end of the conversation Mrs. Coolidge said she had wanted John to join them at White Pine Camp but did not know whether the president would permit it.

John did arrive at White Pine Camp on August 15, from military training at Plattsburgh. He and Boone played tennis, swam, boated on the lake, and hiked. John's mother wanted him beside her as much as possible, seeming to feast on the sight of him. It was a relief to Boone to see the glow in her eyes. When she joined her son and physician for a swim in Osgood Pond, she was always jolly and full of conversation.

Boone suspected one reason for the president's poor disposition that summer was that he was under strain because of a possible visit by Gov. Alfred E. Smith of New York. Pres. George Washington and the then-governor of Massachusetts had established the precedent that a governor should call on a president who visits his state, but Governor Smith had kept everyone guessing as to whether he would show Coolidge this courtesy; the two were potential rivals in the next presidential election.

On twenty-four-hour notice Governor Smith did arrive at Paul Smith's Hotel accompanied by an entourage, baggage, and, despite Prohibition, a lavish supply of liquor. When Capt. Wilson Brown, the newly designated naval aide and *Mayflower* skipper, delivered the president's luncheon invitation, Smith insisted on receiving it in person while dressed in his undershirt, suspenders dangling.

Boone observed Smith at close range during a news conference. He looked keen and shrewd as he talked harshly in an East Side accent out of the side of his mouth and chewed on a cigar at the same time. He was rough in speech and manner. He seemed in a holiday spirit as he shared his liquor with the newspapermen, laughing uproariously and trying to get into as many pictures as possible.

The president was much relieved when the governor departed. He was in such a good frame of mind that when he caught a four-pound pike next day he sent it live to Governor

Smith at Paul Smith's Hotel. The governor responded graciously by saying, "Any fish caught by the president of the United States is quite a distinguished fish. I shall have it cooked for breakfast and shall eat it all alone."[9]

But the presence of the governor at the camp and even the eventual presence of John Coolidge could not disguise a familial problem that Boone knew about by this time, 1926, and which he often thought about. The problem was that President Coolidge essentially was a difficult husband and father. Mrs. Coolidge had gained so much confidence in Boone that she shared intimate details of family affairs. She told him the president had a long history of difficulty in controlling his temper and that when he concentrated intently, such as during preparation of a speech, he became impatient and irritable. Early in married life she had become aware of her husband's peculiarities and realized that she must decide whether she could not tolerate his temperament and terminate the marriage or, alternatively, recognize that she loved him so deeply she would make the best of his frailties, stand by him, and help him in every way she could so long as they lived. She chose the latter course and in doing so learned to become a "safety valve" for her mate.

Mrs. Coolidge's account was confirmed independently by Mrs. Stearns, who confided that the Coolidges as a young couple had many disagreements, with strong opinions voiced on each side. The strength of their ties was not enhanced by the attitude of Grace's mother, Mrs. Goodhue, who had disapproved of the marriage. Boone noted that in contrast to the president, Mrs. Coolidge had the disposition of an angel, but even she had a limit to her patience and her husband knew it.

Boone was a witness to an unhappy incident involving President and Mrs. Coolidge. One day the latter decided she would like to start horseback riding regularly, as Boone and her boys did. She bought a riding outfit including breeches, boots, jacket, and hat, and looking attractive in the new habit, she sauntered into the president's bedroom to surprise him. Boone was there when Coolidge, furious, told her to take off the apparel and never again let him see her in it. Heartbroken, Mrs. Coolidge complied.

Another insight on the president's personality, shared with

Boone by Captain Andrews, the *Mayflower*'s commanding officer, was Andrews's comment that he found it difficult to serve Coolidge, feeling he was changeable and inconsiderate, but that he could not help but like the man.

Mrs. Coolidge was much more of a "social animal" than her husband. She would have enjoyed entertaining young people of John's age aboard the *Mayflower*, with music, dancing, and movies, but when she proposed this to the president he would say, "What for? To spoil them?" One time she suggested that she and John make a cruise on the *Mayflower* while her husband was visiting his father in Plymouth, but he replied that to make the trip while John was home from school would not be good for him and that he must study.

The summer of 1926 in the Adirondacks was not a happy time for the Coolidges. For Boone it was quite pleasant except for the protracted separation from Helen and Suzanne. He had a good time, hiking, fishing, swimming, and golfing. He enjoyed meeting such friends of the Coolidges as the Edsel Fords and Mrs. Whitelaw Reid, the latter the widow of the owner of the *New York Herald Tribune*. When the Fords arrived in their private railroad car, Boone found them natural, unassuming people. He treated Mrs. Ford for a sore throat. For this naval medical officer, who grew up in the anthracite coal region of Pennsylvania, dining on Sunday, August 1, at Mrs. Reid's "summer camp" on Upper St. Regis Lake was an unforgettable experience. After church at St. John's-in-the-Woods, in company with his hostess, he was taken by speedboat to the main cottage. Entering the drawing room, he felt as though he were in a New York City town house. The dining room, with exquisite furnishings, looked like pictures of European palaces, with footmen in white stockings, pink silk breeches, and tail coats. Before each place at the table were a gold-edged place card and a printed menu in French. Boone felt fortunate that he did not have to translate the menu, since the seven courses were served automatically. He found that as soon as he would lay down a fork, a footman whisked the plate away. After the first course Boone learned to keep a finger on the plate until finished with it. This elaborate "camp" was a remarkable contrast to the Coolidges' own simple lifestyle.

Boone was invited back to Mrs. Reid's on several Sundays to play tennis. The first time he and Kermit Roosevelt, son of Pres. Theodore Roosevelt, defeated in doubles the noted tennis star Miss Goss and her sister. The next time, beaten badly by the star in singles, Boone claimed that he had been framed by Carter Field, a newspaperman "friend" who arranged the match.

On the *Mayflower*, Captains Andrews and Brown, successive commanding officers, did their best to entertain. Andrews enhanced Coolidge's enjoyment of the *Mayflower* in a small way by purchasing for him at his own expense at Brooks Brothers—a store too expensive for the president's taste—a yachtsman's cap bearing the gold-embroidered insignia of the president of the United States. Each time the president came aboard, a specially assigned orderly would hand him the cap, and Coolidge would immediately place it on his head, where it remained for the duration of the cruise.

The president had never served in a military capacity and found it awkward to salute. He was not familiar with navy lingo, and this was a secret source of amusement to the ship's officers and men. As commander-in-chief of the army and navy, he was the senior officer present, and it was necessary, therefore, to seek his permission to authorize certain events of the day. As the noon hour approached, an orderly would go up to the president and, standing at rigid salute, ask permission to strike eight bells. The correct reply would have been, "Make it so," but the president's response was invariably, "Aye, aye, sir," which is properly only the reply of a subordinate.[10]

On one cruise of the *Mayflower* the president's father, Col. John Coolidge of Plymouth, was a guest. He was a tall, dignified man with large ears, high forehead, and clear eyes, who had come from the soil of Vermont and seemed carved out of that state's granite. The colonel reportedly had some Native American blood in him. He was the sort of man you would look at twice; his face indicated he had lived long, and when his mind was tapped, information from the school of practical experience would come rolling forth. On Colonel Coolidge's first evening on the *Mayflower* the president asked Boone to assist his father in dressing for dinner and told him that in a closet in the colonel's stateroom he would find a new tuxedo, stiff-bosom dress shirt, dress cuff links and studs, and a black bow tie—all purchased by the president unbeknownst to his father. When Boone instructed the colonel how to put on the shirt and tuxedo and assisted with the bow tie, he took the whole thing as a matter of course and without protest, even though this was a new experience. Without glancing in the mirror, he strode out of his stateroom and went abovedeck to greet other dinner guests. One might have thought he had dressed in a tuxedo every night of his life. He was a handsome figure, and when the president saw him a glint in the eye signified admiration even though not a word was spoken.

On this same cruise down the Potomac, Boone could not help overhearing a conversation between the president and his father as they sat on the main deck watching the scenery. After a long period of silence, the president said in his twang and without looking toward his father, "How is the sheep business?"

Not turning his head toward his son, the father replied, "Good."

A long pause, and the president inquired, "What are they bringing the pound?"[11]

Another period of silence and the colonel cited a price for the sheep.

The exchange continued for so long as Boone was able to observe. Father and son knew each other and the way of Vermont so well that few words and much silence served as communication.

Many years later Boone found the president's son John to have a striking resemblance to his grandfather. On a visit to John in Plymouth he carefully studied a bronze bust of Colonel Coolidge on the mantel, turned it from full face to profile, and asked John to stand alongside, facing the same direction. Boone said he never had seen such a likeness between grandfather and grandson, evident in eyes, eyebrows, nose, and lips.

During the cruises of the latter 1920s, Boone observed that the president had few close friends and suspected that while growing up he had none outside the family. It was an interesting example of how boyhood had molded the man, how rural Vermont could not be removed from even a president of the United States. At times Coolidge would share thoughts with Boone. In a chatty mood one evening he seemed to pat himself on the back, saying that he believed the American people wanted quiet and simplicity in government affairs. Boone felt he was the ideal president for the times because he was able to sit in the boat without rocking it, at the same time inspiring confidence.

For a man with a normally straight face and few words Coolidge could display humor. Boone was present at the White House Correspondents Association dinner at the Mayflower Hotel on March 21, 1926, when the president made an address that showed a markedly human side, a sense of humor evident to few people. He did know how to laugh and enjoyed stories. He did not seem to mind being mimicked and never evidenced bitterness over cartoons or critical things said about him.

Typical of the humor was the way he dealt with former secretary of state Charles E. Hughes as an overnight guest at the White House. A one-time governor of New York, presidential candidate in 1916, secretary of state, and currently a justice of the International Court at The Hague, Hughes was destined to become Chief Justice of the Supreme Court. He wore a distinguishing mark: a full beard and mustache. The first morning after Hughes's arrival, at about breakfast time, the president rang for the White House doorman and presidential barber, Mays, who appeared in white starched coat, carrying a towel draped over his arm and a box containing barber tools. The president said to Mays, "I do not want any haircut or shave, but I want you to go up ... to the bedroom which is being occupied by Justice Hughes. Knock on the door and ask him if he doesn't want a shave."[12] The president insisted Mays go through the routine each morning that Hughes remained as a guest. The chief executive enjoyed being a tease, but Boone doubted that Hughes appreciated the humor.

The president's humor showed in his attitude toward formal White House receptions. Boone and other staff members felt that guests were herded like cattle into the dining room just to be "milked" through a receiving line. Boone remembered how a sweet little woman in a black silk dress adorned with lace collar and cuffs approached the president, curtsied, and said, "You know, Mr. President, I am from Boston." Eyes focused not on the lady but on the next person in line, Coolidge took her hand, pulled it along, and said, in his nasal twang, "Madam, you will never get over it." When Mrs. Stearns asked Coolidge whether this story was true, his response was: "You can vouch for it."[13]

Following one reception for the army and navy, Coolidge greeted 2,360 guests in one hour and five minutes, at the rate of 1.65 seconds per guest. Coming up to the second floor after the reception, the president laughed heartily and boasted of the record he had set.

Boone had been part of an amusing incident involving President and Mrs. Coolidge. As the president was dressing for dinner in Boone's presence, he said to his acting valet, "Dowling, get those new Stacey Adams shoes out of the closet. I want to see if they will fit little Dr. Boone." Dowling got the shoes out and took the trees out of them.

The president said, "Try them on, Doctor!"

They were high-laced shoes, commonly worn in those days. Boone put the right shoe on and, at the president's direction, walked up and down. It pinched a bit, but he did not complain. After all, a gift was coming his way.

Then the president said, "Now you better try on the left one . . . Your feet might be a different size, which they usually are." Boone put on the left shoe and strutted up and down with both shoes. The president asked, "How do they fit, Doctor?"

The reply was, "Fine, Mr. President."

"Well, if they fit you all right, you may have them," said he.

As he thanked the president, Boone took off the shoes and reached over to put the trees in them.

With this, the president speaking more rapidly than usual, said, "Dowling, get those shoe trees away from Docky Boone! Afraid he'll take those shoe trees away with him, also."

Dowling wrapped the shoes and as Boone carried them under his arm he encountered Mrs. Coolidge on the stairway on her way down to dinner. With a smile at the package she said, "Joel, it looks like you have had a windfall."

"Yes, Mrs. Coolidge, the president just gave me a pair of his shoes." Quick as a flash, she said, "Mighty few people can step into the president's shoes!"[14]

6

Passing of the Coolidge Years

For the presidential family, and to some extent the Boone family, the years passed with the presidential summer visits to Swampscott in 1925, the Adirondacks in 1926, the Black Hills in 1927, and a camp on the Brule River in Wisconsin in 1928. For the rest of it, leisure had to be taken aboard the presidential yacht, which President and Mrs. Coolidge thoroughly enjoyed. Both seemed relaxed and happier there than when in the more formal surroundings of the White House. To the best of Boone's knowledge President Coolidge never brought work with him.

1

Helen and Joel were thrilled by the Christmas gift they received from the Coolidges' friends the Stearnses in 1927: an invitation to a cruise of the Caribbean. The new year had promised to be pleasant, beginning with the usual elaborate party at the Ned McLeans', the wealthy couple they had met through the Hardings. During the Caribbean trip with the Stearnses on the United Fruit Company steamer *Santa Rosa*, the Boones visited Cuba, Jamaica, Panama, and Costa Rica, where they were entertained by the diplomatic corps, since it was common knowledge that Stearns was President Coolidge's political mentor.

Stearns was a fanatic on the subject of Prohibition, generally refusing a drink even when outside the jurisdiction of the United States, as on the British-registered *Santa Rosa*. It was therefore with amusement that Boone told the story of their visit in Costa Rica. When a large tray of predinner drinks of all kinds was passed, Stearns was the only one to abstain; he was unaccustomed to drinking anything. At dinner he did decide to taste the champagne. It must have tasted good, for rather than sipping it he would empty his glass in one or two swallows as soon as it had been replenished by the butler. Before dessert was served, Stearns's head drooped with his chin resting on the bosom of his dress shirt. He had fallen asleep.

Stearns suffered a good bit of seasickness. When told of it, President Coolidge broke into a smile. He was glad to find one more thing that he and his old friend had in common.

Perhaps the high point of the cruise was at Havana. AT&T offered the Boones an opportunity to place a call to Suzanne without charge. This was the first time they had ever talked on the telephone from one country to another.

On the way home Boone enjoyed discussing the question as to whether President Coolidge should run for reelection in 1928. The consensus was that he should not run because if he did he would find the electorate tired of him. Boone felt there was bound to be a reaction to Coolidge's conservatism, so extreme as to bring a radical successor within another four years. Little did he know how prescient this observation was.

Not all of Boone's conversations with Stearns were so agreeable, although he restrained himself out of respect for his friend and patient, who was overweight and short of breath, who overate, oversmoked, and suffered hypertension, and whose idea of exercise was sitting in a rocking chair. Boone could hardly contain himself when the older man complained that Secretary of Commerce Hoover was upstaging Coolidge and seeking nomination for the presidency. Stearns said the Republican Party could not nominate Hoover and, if he was nominated, could not elect him. He accused Hoover of being insensitive. Boone's unspoken reaction: "Stearns was far off base on all counts!"

The Stearnses proved extremely kind to the Boone family. Helen and Suzanne spent several summers at their Swampscott summer house, Red Gables. In those pre-air-conditioning days the opportunity to exchange the heat and humidity of Washington for the breezes of the New England seashore was a godsend.

With President and Mrs. Coolidge accompanied by Dr.

Coupal planning to spend the summer of 1927 in the Black Hills, the arrangement was for Boone to remain with the *Mayflower*, a prospect he found pleasing since the ship was scheduled to be in New England waters. On June 11 all three Boones were on board to witness Charles A. Lindbergh's triumphant return from France aboard the USS *Memphis*. "Lindy" had recently completed his historic transatlantic flight, the first of its kind, from Long Island to Paris. Boone became well acquainted with Lindbergh, beginning with a Coolidge reception held just a few days after his return.

When it came time for the *Mayflower* to sail for the Boston Navy Yard, Helen and Suzanne accompanied Joel. At the age of seven, Suzanne was a great little sailor, according to her father, concerned that the fuss made over her might spoil the child. She was the only child to sail aboard the *Mayflower* in that ship's fifty years of service, so far as Boone was able to determine. Upon arrival the Boones enjoyed a pleasant summer with the Stearnses and friends in Swampscott and Marblehead, with swimming and sailing.

Boone continued to hear critical comments from his friends about an incident the previous summer. The *Mayflower* had up-anchored and steamed through a group of sailboats in the midst of a race, creating a sizable wake and turmoil, although no one was injured and no boats damaged. President Coolidge had suddenly decided he wanted to leave Marblehead, and Captain Andrews took his orders literally.

Before return to Washington on August 1, Boone had another talk with Stearns about his extended tour of duty in Washington. Unbeknownst to him, it was to lead into trouble, although everything turned out all right. Coolidge's confidant began the subject by giving Boone the opinion that it would be better to get out of the navy: "If you stay another ten years, you won't be worth anything professionally or personally." He advised him to go into private practice. Taking this advice to heart, Boone responded by saying, "I will not remain beyond March 29 [1928] under any circumstances that I can foresee."[1] Telling of this conversation in later years, he acknowledged he had been a bit shortsighted.

The talk caused Boone to think about his current job. There was, of course, the prestige associated with serving the chief executive and First Lady, the glamour of rubbing shoulders with national figures. Mrs. Coolidge made a point of seeing to it that the Boones were included in White House social activities, such as festivities surrounding the Christmas season—listening to carols on Christmas Eve and joining the president, First Lady, and cabinet secretaries and wives at the New Year's receptions for thousands of guests in the Blue Room.

Boone was intrigued by the *Mayflower*'s guests, mingling on a single cruise with General Pershing, Major General Lejeune, and Secretary of State Kellogg. He never forgot a comment by Pershing, the foremost American military man of the day. He said "some people are 'hipped' on aviation," but went on to say that infantry and battleships would continue to be the paramount resources of the army and navy.[2] Lejeune had commanded the Second Division, in which Boone served and was commandant of the Marine Corps. Kellogg succeeded Hughes as secretary of state in 1925.

Another *Mayflower* guest Boone remembered particularly well was the president's Aunt Sarah Pollard from Vermont, who was probably on her first visit to Washington. Boone watched as Coolidge escorted his aunt up the gangway. As soon as the president stepped on deck the band struck up the national anthem and Coolidge doffed his hat, held it over his heart, and stood at attention. Boone observed the aunt looking up at her nephew in amazement and saying in her Vermont way, "Cal, this can't be for you, is it?" His eyes straight ahead, the president said under his breath, "No, it's not for me personally, but for the office of the president of the United States, and I have the greatest respect for the presidency."[3]

Boone's job carried such perquisites as use of the White House tennis courts, army stables, and the *Mayflower*. One of the more memorable parties on the *Mayflower* was held on May 26, 1927, in celebration of Suzanne's seventh birthday. Sixty children were present, along with Mrs. Coolidge and Mrs. Stearns. The First Lady provided flowers and decorations for the dining room. The children had the run of the ship, which resounded with merriment. For years afterward the Boones would hear that there had never been such a party as Suzanne's aboard the yacht. Suzanne liked to tell how the steward had introduced animation by placing live baby ducks in a pool in the middle of the table—a decoration her father found objectionable for sanitary reasons.

Perhaps the close and enduring friendship that developed between the Boones—Helen, Joel and Suzanne—and Mrs. Coolidge was the most rewarding feature of Boone's White House assignment. "Suzanne Spends a Night at the White House," mentioned earlier, was followed by other notes from that First Lady. Helen and Joel carried on a correspondence with her for so long as she lived—she died in 1957. Suzanne came to possess a bundle of letters by Mrs. Coolidge, each revealing what a gracious person she was, what interest she had in family and friends.

At the same time there were the requirements on a presidential physician, who had to see not merely the president and his family but also other individuals in the government. His clientele included the White House staff, officers and men of the *Mayflower* and families, and cabinet members and families.

One of Boone's more troubling cases was that of Secretary of Agriculture Henry C. Wallace, whom Boone described as "a very likable gentleman." Wallace had been with President Harding on the trip to Alaska in 1923 and was from Des Moines, where he had succeeded his father as owner and editor of *Wallaces' Farmer*, the largest of the nation's farm journals. In September 1924, after X rays and consultations, Wallace was operated on at the naval hospital for removal of his gallbladder and appendix. Following what appeared to be a satisfactory recovery, the doctors became anxious and then alarmed. Wallace died on October 25. The cause was bacteremia, the contributing cause cholecystitis, or inflammation of the gallbladder. As reported in the newspapers, Boone was the only person with the secretary during his last hours. As Wallace lay dying, Boone began to whistle the Iowa song "Out Where the Tall Corn Grows," which the secretary had taught him on the Alaska trip. This roused Wallace, who moved his lips in song and raised his arm in salute to his beloved state. He never regained consciousness.

Years later, recalling his White House experiences and the loss of a third patient of prominence in the space of fourteen months, Boone had this to say: "Once . . . again I suffered a horrible, horrible shock . . . I had had excellent colleagues associated with me for the most part, but I didn't have available the medical knowledge . . . operating procedures . . . medications . . . forms of therapy . . . that other physicians had many years later. Would that I could retrace my professional journey . . . "[4]

Boone took his responsibilities seriously and was subject to call at any time. Helen was likely to be called on short notice to fill in for a guest unable to appear at a White House function, for with her outgoing personality, knowledge of affairs, and sense of humor she was a welcome addition. But as stimulating as this life was, it made almost inordinate demands. Joel had little time; even while off duty he was likely to be riding or playing tennis with John Coolidge, members of the White House staff, or guests. Opportunities to play with Suzanne—which brought to mind Joel's youth and his tomboy girlfriend Helen—were all too rare. A lieutenant commander's salary—the Boones' only income—was hardly adequate to cover social obligations and a wardrobe suitable for all occasions. Frugality was a necessity; at Christmas the only presents exchanged were such practical items as a set of automobile tires. President Coolidge's Yankee thriftiness contributed to balancing the federal budget but made life difficult for people who traveled with him. They were privileged to accompany him, and no other compensation was necessary, according to the president's secretary, Ted Clark.

As 1928 neared, Boone became concerned about Coupal's status at the White House and his relationship to it. Mrs. Coolidge had complained that Coupal never seemed around when she needed him, even when she ran a fishhook into her hand. Boone once was called away from the Chevy Chase Club to treat the president's throat, even though Coupal was at the White House; the president insisted on Boone. Not long afterward the president scratched Coupal's name and substituted Boone's on a list of people to accompany him during a trip to Philadelphia.

The timing of Coupal's fall from favor was curious inasmuch as a bill was pending in Congress that would have promoted him to colonel. Would the promotion be temporary? Would the bill apply to Boone? He tried to discuss it with one of the presidential secretaries, Everett Sanders, who became irritated, told him he should stay out of the matter, and gratuitously added that the Hardings had done nothing for Boone's advancement. Baffled by Sanders, whom Boone considered a friend, he was unwilling to drop the matter. He discussed it with the surgeon general of the navy, the judge advocate general, the chief of the bureau of Navigation, and the secretary of the navy. His own views were that any promotion of a White House physician based on the position held should be temporary, covering the expenses incurred holding the post, and the bill should apply equally to medical officers of the army and navy. His colleagues supported Boone.

He broached the subject with Coolidge—an action he would regret. The president "became furious and certainly did blow his top." He said he did not favor promotion of physicians just because they were assigned to the White House but had approved the temporary promotion of Coupal as a matter of "simple justice." He said that Coupal had been put to expense during summers in Swampscott, the Adirondacks, and Black Hills, while Boone lived aboard the *Mayflower* at Swampscott and in the marine camp in the Adirondacks and had not gone to the Black Hills.

Boone might have been well advised to drop the subject, but told the president that the Navy Department wished equal treatment to that proposed for the army. With that Coolidge said the surgeon general had better not presume to question the wisdom of his actions or he "would get himself into trouble." The president's face turned a brilliant red, and he turned on his heel and left. Coolidge returned in a few minutes and said calmly, "Doctor, I like you personally and your work, but when you wish to discuss government business, make an appointment with Everett Sanders to discuss it with him in his office."[5] Boone had learned a lesson: the president felt entitled to discuss a subject with him anywhere and any time so long as he initiated the conversation, but if Boone wanted to bring up a touchy subject, beware.

Leaving White House with Helen after 1928 New Year's Day reception

The final year of the administration, 1928, began with a trip to Cuba, where the president addressed the Sixth Pan-American Conference. Coolidge enjoyed having the humorist Will Rogers as his guest on the train to Key West. According to Boone, who along with Coupal accompanied the party, the president was fond of Rogers's storytelling; the two men sat together for hours, much to the president's amusement. Boone felt this form of relaxation was therapeutic for a president who worried in advance of a speech such as the one before a crowd in Cuba. At such a time, he could become irritable and excited and lose his temper.

A disruption occurred on the train when Coupal broke the compressor hose on the tank used to spray the president's throat. The president complained to Boone that Coupal was always breaking everything, saying, "You should not permit him to handle any of your therapy gear."[6]

After returning from Cuba, Boone was involved in treating Mrs. Coolidge and her mother, Mrs. Goodhue, who lived in Northampton. Mrs. Coolidge suffered from chronic fatigue, while her mother had an abdominal mass presumed to be malignant.

In Mrs. Coolidge's case, Boone consulted not only Coupal but also Dr. Young at Johns Hopkins. On February 8 he took Mrs. Coolidge to the naval hospital in his car, without a Secret Service man, so as not to be seen by press representatives. There an examination by Young and an assistant, Dr. Scott, revealed through both a cystoscopy and X rays that Mrs. Coolidge had an enlarged and misplaced right kidney, with obstruction to its drainage. In the meantime, animal inoculation tests had begun for signs of infection. Boone explained to the president that his wife might have contracted an infection and removal of one kidney might become necessary. The next day when the president asked how the "little pigs" were getting along and whether they showed any "temperature," Boone worriedly had to tell him that the guinea pigs were showing pathology of an indeterminate nature.

Because Mrs. Coolidge was in pain, Boone spent days and

nights at the White House. When he and Coupal favored different therapies, the president sided with Boone, saying, "You know best." Young endorsed Boone's course. When Boone told a consultant in internal medicine, Dr. Walter Bloedorn, that Coupal had suggested heart stimulants, Bloedorn said, "No! Don't let them stampede you. Use your own judgment."[7]

As Mrs. Coolidge was struggling with illness, her mother grew weaker. As soon as Mrs. Coolidge regained strength, she and Boone made the first of what proved three trips to Northampton. They stayed in the house at 21 Massasoit Street, where the family had lived since 1906, until the head of the household went to Washington as vice president. "It was a comfortable house though not large, . . . simply furnished," Boone recalled, contrasting it with living quarters at the White House.[8] There was one bathroom. Boone occupied the room on the second floor in which John and Calvin, Jr., had been born.

Despite being underweight and short of sleep, the First Lady insisted on these trips. A compensation was that along with Boone, she could see John, enrolled at Amherst College, and become better acquainted with John's fiancée, Florence Trumbull, and her parents, Governor and Mrs. Trumbull of Plainville, Connecticut.

On the third trip John told his mother that he did not see how she put up living with his father. They had just had an altercation. John went on to say he had just told his good friend Jack Hills of his worries that as he grew older his own disposition might be getting to be more like his father's.[9]

In Northampton on Sunday, March 4, 1928, Mrs. Coolidge telephoned the president to say, "Just wanted to remind you we have but one more year, Calvin."[10] She could hardly wait to return to Northampton, far removed from the demands of officialdom.

All the while life continued in the White House; as the months passed, the president's duties, political and ceremonial, could hardly stop. Boone moved between Washington and Northampton but spent most of his time in the capital, where every time the president had a reception for the diplomatic corps or whatever it was necessary for him to be on hand.

By Memorial Day, with the approach of the Republican national convention, there was much discussion in White House circles about whether President Coolidge would be offered the nomination, despite his statement the previous summer that "I do not choose to run." The question of health was raised. J. Russell Young of the *Washington Star* stated that Coolidge was in better health than when he took office. Boone did not concur with a view attributed to Dr. Coupal that the president did not even need a physician. He needed one very much, Boone felt, since he did have indispositions and was prone to make frequent calls for his physician. Boone took exception to reporter Young's claim that Coolidge was a "rugged" individual, for his body was "firm of texture, but it was not particularly strong muscular development." Coolidge had worked on a farm but not been an athlete. Young was off base when he said the president "has a talent for not getting excited or worrying." The truth was he worried a great deal. When Young said that the president "has the strength to endure physical strains . . . and he is not the kind to tire easily as the result of unusual physical exertion," Boone again disagreed, saying Coolidge "tired very readily, mentally and physically, and required a great deal of sleep, long naps in the daytime and long hours in bed at night."[11]

Boone's conviction that Coolidge was not rugged was sadly confirmed by his death at age sixty in 1933, less than four years after he left the White House.

Mrs. Coolidge's health became a campaign issue. On the *Mayflower*, June 2, Thomas Cochran, a New York City banker, and Dwight W. Morrow approached Boone. Morrow was an Amherst classmate of the president, ambassador to Mexico, and future father-in-law of Charles A. Lindbergh. These men urged Boone to issue a statement that Mrs. Coolidge's health would not bar the president's nomination. He refused, knowing Mrs. Coolidge was not well and wanted release from White House life. This displeased Morrow and Cochran, but Boone recognized his obligation as a physician. He never regretted that position, feeling that if he had been willing to see Mrs. Coolidge's life sacrificed during another four years in the White House he would have been unable to forgive himself.

Soon thereafter, Boone's concern for Mrs. Coolidge became acute. Upon return from leave on June 8 he was shocked by the First Lady's condition. Her kidney trouble had returned, and she looked drawn and pallid. It was obvious that she had been heavily medicated, for she looked as though she had been doped, with a dry mouth and unnatural stare. When he attempted to review her condition with Coupal the following morning, Coupal was loathe to talk. Boone did learn that Coupal had failed to follow the instruction that in event of recurrence he should consult Dr. Young and administer only local treatment. Boone thought to himself, *Oh, God, what a way to practice medicine!*[12]

At this time Coolidge became terribly upset not only because of his wife's condition but also because of another distraction. Coolidge adored his wife, considered her the center of his life, and thought of her almost all the time, even though he often said little about her health or illness and gave the impression he did not care. The prospect of serious illness was almost more than he could bear. Then there was the prospect of the Republican national convention, scheduled to open on June 12 in Kansas City. He was anxious to be out of Washington during the convention, headed for the Brule River in Wisconsin, where he had decided to spend the summer, despite his wife's desire not to be far from her mother. Boone likened the president's behavior to that of a caged lion and feared temperamental derangement, realizing that he had not two, but three patients. For two days departure for Wisconsin was delayed because of Mrs. Coolidge's high fever. The delay increased the president's restiveness. Coolidge suffered from a sore heel and did not wish to see anyone as he hobbled about the bedroom. Mrs. Coolidge's somewhat offhand comment concerning the sore heel was, "The elephant must have stepped on it."[13]

The Coolidges and entourage left for Wisconsin on June 13, after Boone advised the president that Mrs. Coolidge should go to the Mayo Clinic if her condition did not improve. It had been decided that he would not accompany the presidential party, so he would be close enough to go to Northampton in event of an emergency with Mrs. Goodhue.

The scene shifted to the convention, and Boone found himself in the middle of discussions of the president's enigmatic behavior toward it. He concluded that the president might have been willing to run again if "drafted" and was disappointed not to have been consulted concerning the nomination of Hoover. Secretary of the Interior Work, about to be named chairman of the national committee, explained that the party could not afford the risk that Coolidge would turn down the nomination and by doing so make the eventual nominee appear a "second-rater." When Boone told Work that individuals close to the president felt he would accept if no one else was competent, he snorted. Stearns had no use for Hoover, was bitter over the nomination, and said the president long ago should have removed both Hoover and Work from his cabinet.

During a pleasant summer with Helen and Suzanne, cruising to New England on the *Mayflower*, staying again with the Stearnses at Swampscott, Boone was gratified to learn from letters from Mrs. Coolidge that the summer in Wisconsin had done wonders for her health. Knowing she would relinquish the position of First Lady on March 4, 1929, was a factor in her recovery. For all this Mrs. Coolidge gave Boone credit. Writing to a friend, she said, "As for Dr. Boone, he has full-grown wings, but I hope they will not let him fly away from me."[14]

In such ways, with all the worries and sometimes the disorder of those last years, 1927 and 1928, the tour of duty at the White House during the Coolidge era began to move toward its close. To an outside observer everything must have seemed almost on a grand scale, with Boone having access to the leaders of government including the president and Mrs. Coolidge. He associated with world-famous individuals in diverse fields of endeavor—the arts, science, industry, finance, entertainment, sports and politics. When he wished, he and the family might sail on the *Mayflower*, and a birthday party for Suzanne saw not merely dozens of guests but also inclusion of the First Lady. The receptions for the diplomatic corps and other huge groups of Washington officialdom, with all the glitter of the occasions, might have made Boone's fellow naval officers envious. Having evolved into a gregarious person and ardent letter writer, Boone took the opportunity to make dozens of friends, many of whom he kept in touch with over the years to follow. And yet there was the other side of the equation, in that he worried day and night over the health of his charges and worried also about his career, which was virtually becoming endangered by such a long tour of duty in one billet, one that qualified technically as sea duty but was far removed from the fighting navy.

It seems life in or near the White House carried liabilities and confusion that was foreign to Boone's orderly approach to life. The rewards were large. But so were the responsibilities.

7

Transition to a New President

The three presidents of the 1920s and early 1930s—Harding, Coolidge, and Hoover—were as different as they could be, and the decade and more Boone spent in the White House during their administrations might have seemed to him three different assignments, as he remained while White House inhabitants came and went. It was a great experience, to be sure, not of a sort presented to many army or navy officers. No single individual, it seems safe to say, saw these presidents more than did Boone. If he could have lived his life over again, he never would have given up the experience, even in favor of duty he so enjoyed with the marines or at sea. For the rest of his life he looked back on his conversations and confidences with the presidents of that now long-gone era

Of the three presidents he knew so well, Hoover was probably the individual Boone liked the most. He was the presidential physician to Hoover, and not an assistant as during the Harding and Coolidge administrations. There was also a personal bond not present during the earlier period. Harding was easy to get along with and yet was dignified and kept his distance. Coolidge was sui generis, always a little on the difficult side, sometimes remarkably so. Hoover might have seemed an unlikely individual with whom to share anything, for he was reported to be dour and thereby, so outsiders presumed, difficult. In fact, Boone found him quite the opposite.

1

In the waning days of the Coolidge administration Boone

began to wonder how the forthcoming election would affect his career. Although acknowledging that some of his brother officers on the *Mayflower* would have preferred Al Smith because he wanted to do away with Prohibition, Boone was pleased when Hoover was elected president. Boone had known Hoover as secretary of commerce in the Harding and Coolidge administrations. He recently had had a conversation with Mrs. Hoover about a preparatory school for her nephew that led to enrollment at Boone's beloved Mercersburg Academy, paralleling the experience that six years earlier had brought him close to Mrs. Coolidge. But it was the opportunity to accompany the Hoovers on a preinauguration goodwill visit to South America—the first such visit of any president or president-elect—that provided an opening to become well acquainted with the about-to-be First Family.

The trip to South America was exhilarating. On board the battleship *Maryland* (President Coolidge had attempted to substitute a cruiser because "it would not cost so much"), Boone participated in the social activities and was treated royally. In Brazil he was quartered in the presidential palace and to his amusement addressed as "Sr. Capitan de Fragata Boone." He spent time with both Mr. and Mrs. Hoover. Boone recalled standing on the main deck with Mrs. Hoover as her younger son Allan, looking pale, emerged from below. Worried, Mrs. Hoover turned to Boone and said, "Doctor, Allan always feels any slight motion of a ship. See how pale he is. He's going to become sick. Take him down below and get him to lie down on one of the beds."[1] Boone could not help chortling to himself. The ship was not making the slightest motion, and he knew Allan and friends had been partying all night in Buenos Aires.

Boone had this to say about his conversations with Hoover on the cruise home aboard the battleship *Utah*: "He seemed to know a good deal about my naval career and asked many questions about it. He was one of the most fascinating conversationalists I have ever met. Yet at times we maintained long periods of silence as we walked the decks together, attributable perhaps to our common Quaker background."[2]

It was on the *Utah* that Boone first noticed that Hoover, at

President Hoover and cabinet playing "Hoover Ball" as invented by Boone

five-eleven and 210 pounds, was overweight and in need of more strenuous physical exercise than walking—which he did often, frequently arm-in-arm with Mrs. Hoover. Boone persuaded him to join other players in exercising with a medicine ball about the size of a volleyball and weighing anywhere from four to fifteen pounds. At first the players—Hoover, Boone, the newspaperman Mark Sullivan, and others—stood in a circle and passed a nine-pound ball. Drawing on experience with deck tennis, Boone devised a game in which the ball was thrown across a net within a court marked with chalk. This was a forerunner of the medicine ball game played by Hoover on the White House grounds that made such an important contribution to his health.

By this time the trip was almost over. Hoover was becoming restless. He was anxious to select his cabinet, make other appointments, and organize the administration.

The last edition of the *Utah*'s newspaper, the *Evening Bulletin*, distributed January 5, 1933, included a report from Washington that President Coolidge had recommended $5,000 to purchase an automobile for the incoming vice president, Sen. Charles Curtis, with provision that Vice President Dawes's machine be traded in.

Upon return Boone watched the administration spend its last weeks and days to inaugurate the new. He and other officers of the *Mayflower* were delighted to have Mrs. Coolidge as their guest for luncheon on Sunday, February 17, 1929. This was probably the first time a First Lady had been the sole guest of the wardroom mess. Mrs. Coolidge brought an iron Scottie dog bearing a tag on which she had written an amusing piece of doggerel:

Within This Room

Hark, hark, the dogs do bark,
The Hoovers are coming to town.
The Coolidges depart
With a pain in the heart
And Congress looks down with a frown.
The city is dressed in its beautiful best,
The Avenue bristles with seats
The *Mayflower* rocks

At the Navy Yard docks
While we laugh and partake of the eats.

[signed] Only, a dog[3]

The Scottie was given to Suzanne. Years later she remembered that "pretending the Scottie to be real, I often dragged it by a leash around our apartment, while Mother scolded me for scratching the hardwood floors."[4] Now the Scottie rests on a Vermont hearth where Helen and Joel Boone's great-grandchildren try to ride it as if it were a horse.

Boone's contacts with the Hoovers resumed on February 23 when Hoover's valet, Kostos Boris, called to say that Mrs. Hoover wished to see him. Upon arriving at the "S" Street house he joined her and her secretary, Ruth Fesler, in the upstairs living quarters. Mrs. Hoover had sent for him because Miss Fesler was ill with a sore throat and fever and as a Christian Scientist refused to accept treatment. Boone's solution was simple: send her into the country with Christian Science friends until her infection disappeared.

Before he could leave he learned that Hoover wished to see him. After treating Hoover for a cold, Boone was on his way out when Hoover's secretary, George Akerson, whispered that he was to be named "Physician to the President" but must say nothing to anyone until Hoover, himself, gave the word. The day before, Boone had heard through Ted Clark that he would be staying on at the White House and there would be no assignment for Coupal.

For days Boone was on tenterhooks as he awaited word from Hoover. Finally, March 1, Hoover sent for him, greeted him cordially, and, inviting him to sit down, said he wanted Boone to become his physician.

"Sir, I do not wish to be impertinent," Boone responded, " but does this mean that I would serve in co-association with some other physician?"

"No, but why do you ask?"

"Mr. Hoover, for seven years I have been serving in co-association with two other physicians assigned at different times to the White House. For me, this has been a most unsatisfactory experience as well as one that has been fraught with danger. I am, indeed, highly honored to be asked to serve as your physician, but I must say that if you had had co-association in mind, I would have been compelled to ask respectfully that you withdraw the proposal."

"No," Hoover said, "I wish to have only one physician, and you are the one I want. I am gratified that you feel as you do and that you have expressed yourself so frankly. I would like you also to continue as physician to the *Mayflower*, but I do not want that to be a burden. I also must tell you in confidence that I am not sure that the *Mayflower* will be retained as the presidential yacht."[5]

The session ended with a handshake accompanied by an expression of thanks and a broad smile from the president-elect. Boone went on his way rejoicing, for at long last he had the prospect of freedom from concern that his every move was being second-guessed by General Sawyer or Major Coupal.

"Inauguration day was upon us before we knew it," Boone recalled. "In the morning I went to the White House living quarters to say good-bye to President and Mrs. Coolidge, and we exchanged warm comments about our lives together. Then Helen and I participated in the formal farewell in the Blue Room along with members of the Coolidge and Hoover cabinets and their wives. Neither Coupal nor his wife was present."[6] At the ceremonies, with rain pouring on them, the Boones—Joel, Helen, and Suzanne—were seated in the presidential box behind Mrs. Coolidge.

The Coolidge years thus came to an end with an assignment that made Boone at long last very happy. He would be his own man. The years with Sawyer had been worrisome, for Boone never could be sure what the little general from Marion might recommend. Harding's doctor, and for a while Coolidge's, was a prescriber of little white pills, of flat pills, of green liquid in a bottle. He would advise presidents to take soda water three times a day. His way of examining patients' hearts was to put his head down and listen to the thumps, rather than use a stethoscope. Boone was not sure that Sawyer, because of his failing vision,

could see anything. In his last months in the White House—
Sawyer died in 1924—the Marion physician was becoming for-
getful and worried about his relations with Coolidge. The latter,
to be sure, did not like him and once told Boone he felt better
when Sawyer was in Marion.

Coupal was something else. He was a family physician of a
sort that one might have discovered in towns and small cities
across the length and breadth of the United States. Being a
younger man, Boone had received the best of instruction at Hahnemann, but many of the older physicians had barely more
training than one might have expected from lawyers of the
time—that is, they practiced on their patients in a literal sense,
albeit usually in the company of older physicians. Until the
1890s many states had no licensing requirements for doctors. In
Ohio all that was necessary for anyone wishing to practice was
for that individual to register his desire with the local probate
court. Coupal was better than that, but Boone feared not much
better, and when he had encountered Mrs. Coolidge staring like
a zombie, so doped by Coupal that she hardly knew what she was
about, he could only remind Coupal of his obligation to have consulted Dr. Young of Johns Hopkins, perhaps the greatest specialist in urology in the country. Coupal evidently considered himself
the next greatest.

At long last, in the Hoover administration, Boone would be
free to make his own diagnoses and watch over his own treatments.

2

That Boone as physician to the White House held only the
rank of lieutenant commander annoyed President Hoover. The
last naval officer to serve in that capacity, Cary Grayson, physician to President Wilson, had been elevated by special legislation
to rear admiral, three grades higher than Boone, albeit
Grayson's advancement ahead of 133 other medical officers had
created widespread resentment within the navy. Hoover made
clear that he wanted his physician to receive at least the same

recognition as Grayson, especially in view of Boone's war record. Boone did not resist a promotion but felt it should be temporary and tied to the position as the president's physician.

Congress passed a bill specifying that, in case of an armed services officer, the rank of a navy captain or army colonel shall attach to the position of physician to the White House. While this action provided relief to Boone's strained family budget, it left him to face the prospect of a reduction to lieutenant commander upon departure from the White House. While in France during the world war he had been promoted temporarily to lieutenant commander, and years later during World War II he was to be advanced temporarily from captain to commodore.

After passage of the legislation a navy selection board met in mid-1931 to select seven medical officers from a field of thirty-three eligible for permanent promotion to the rank of commander. According to Boone, the new surgeon general, Rear Admiral C. E. Riggs, went out of his way to prevent his selection. Riggs interfered with the selection board's independence by telling Rear Admiral Kennedy, the man he had named head of the board, that unless Boone was among those selected, President Hoover probably would disapprove the board's recommendations. Riggs had the audacity to inform Boone that he had told board members "in confidence" that Boone was indifferent as to whether he were to be selected.

Boone was passed over, which may have been the board's way of asserting its independence. Hoover rejected the board's recommendations in toto, marking the first time since Wilson's administration that a chief executive had turned them down. Within six weeks this led to Boone's selection by a second board, but at the same time there was so much publicity that his longer-term interests as a navy officer could have been damaged. Boone considered resigning upon completion of his current assignment.

When the promotion to commander finally came, friends inside and outside the services, including such officers as Gen. Douglas MacArthur, congratulated him. At the same time there is no doubt that the circumstances produced jealousy toward an officer who had been so much in the limelight. How else to explain why this most highly decorated member of the Medical

Department was never to become surgeon general?

The hand of Admiral Riggs was evident throughout the promotion fiasco. One of Boone's friends warned that Riggs was "out to get" him, perhaps because he resented his closeness to Secretary of the Navy Charles Francis Adams and Assistant Secretary Ernest Jahncke. Adams had little use for Riggs, asking Boone one day, "Is he crazy?"[7]

The hostility between Riggs and Boone reached its height when the surgeon general told Boone he felt the first board had acted correctly. "I told Admiral Riggs," Boone recalled, "that I had lost confidence in him personally and officially. I said that loss of confidence was shared by others."[8] Boone went on to tell Riggs that for the good of the Medical Corps he should resign. Riggs turned white as a sheet, said he had no intention of resigning, and accused Boone of bucking for the position of surgeon general. This exchange was followed by Riggs's efforts—unsuccessful—to blackball Boone's application for membership in the Chevy Chase Club.

In his papers Boone took pains to explain that documentation of the events relating to his promotion to commander was based on notes made at the time, not recollections thirty years later. This was one of the most traumatic experiences of his life, the one and only time when he was so thoroughly disenchanted with another human being.

But promotion was a minor problem, one must add, compared to the friendship that rapidly developed between Boone and the new president. With Hoover he discovered a man of his own heart, an individual who was a joy to work with, and with whom he did not have to observe all the formalities and thereby the tensions and awkwardnesses that had marked his relations with Coolidge. Moreover, the new relationship lacked the formalities that affected his medical care of the Hardings (even though President and Mrs. Harding were altogether admirable human beings, with whom Boone got along quite well). It was so pleasant to find that the new president counted upon and looked forward to the association. Boone felt that in a very real way he was a member of the Hoover administration

Within hours after arrival at the White House, following the inaugural ceremonies on March 4, 1929, Boone heard President Hoover say, "I want to go to your office. I have a sore finger."

"Come along with me, Mr. President," he replied. This was the first time he had addressed Hoover as "Mr. President."

He led the president to a linen closet in the center of the long hall on the second floor. After he had opened the double doors, revealing shelves lined with bottles, dressings and medical instruments, Hoover said with a note of annoyance, "But I want to go to your office."

"This is our office," was the reply.

"What do you mean? Is that an office to take care of people in a clinic?"

"No, sir. We doctors considered ourselves very fortunate when we got this cabinet. Until we had that, we had to carry a medicine bag around the White House."

Hoover was astounded to learn that a linen cabinet was the only on-site medical facility for physicians expected to look after the president, his family, staff and guests, as well as other officials. As soon as Boone dressed Hoover's finger he said, "I want you to pick out a room in the White House. You may take any room you wish and establish an office where you can really do your job as a physician to me and to the White House as a whole."

Elated at the prospect of having an adequate facility in the White House, Boone identified a space in the basement used as a pool room during the Cleveland and Wilson administrations. Then he waited for Hoover to ask, "How about that office I asked you to establish? Have you found space that you wish to have for it?"

"Yes, sir, I have found a room."

"Come on; I want to go and see it."

Boone led the president to the nicely furnished basement room, adorned with a large marble fireplace and view of the south grounds through a window framed with a magnolia tree. He imagined placing his desk so he could enjoy that view.

Looking around the room and the adjoining washroom with marble floor and white tiling, the president said, "Well, this looked like a very good office for you, but now where will your clinic be?"

"Oh, I'll do everything in this room."

"Oh, not at all, not at all. Let's you and I look around for another room or rooms. We can have you establish a clinic, as you should have."

Roaming the kitchens and pantries on the north side of the basement, together with Boone, the president paused in one room and asked, "What room is this and what's it used for?"

"This is the valet's room, where he does his pressing . . . Old 'Major' Brooks had this room as his headquarters for many years as a valet; then his successors occupied it. There in the wall to the north you can see a huge safe. That is where the silver of the White House is stored and was under the custody of Brooks . . . until impaired health forced his retirement."

"This would make a good clinic room, wouldn't it, if it's big enough?" said the president.

"Oh, it's plenty big enough."

"Let's then make this the clinic."

"Sir, I would have to walk from my room out into the main lobby of the basement floor around through an archway by the kitchen and then into the auxiliary servants' dining room and into this room."

"Oh, not at all We will just cut a hole through from your office into this room."

"Sir, but, the walls are four feet thick."

"So what? We will just use electric drills and drill through the stone walls, make a doorway."[9] Boone had forgotten that the president was a mining engineer.

The office and adjacent clinic soon became a reality. For the first time a White House physician had been provided with adequate facilities, and for the rest of his life Boone was to be proud of his role in bringing this about. A donated Ritter dental chair became one of the first pieces of equipment installed in the clinic. It proved useful for not only dental work but also eye, ear, nose and throat treatment.

At this stage of the clinic's development, its capabilities were improved but still limited. Although there was a portable electrocardiograph machine, X rays had to be done outside the White House. Laboratory material was sent to the naval medical school. Boone relied on the nearby naval medical dispensary. At first he was the sole member of the White House medical staff, but in response to a request he was delighted when a hospital corpsman, George A. Fox, was reassigned from the dispensary on a full-time basis. Fox was no stranger to the White House, having been called there to assist Grayson during President Wilson's long illness. "Fox was a natural" whom Boone remembered as a cheerful, imaginative individual who could be trusted to act independently in many situations.[10] His wide practical experience in the navy compensated to a large extent for the lack of a degree in medicine. Fox would become well-known in later years for care of President Hoover's successor, the handicapped Franklin Roosevelt.

The White House medical unit soon became a "beehive of activity," as Boone described it. Over a period of sixty-nine years its staff has increased from two to twenty, including four physicians, four registered nurses, and four physician assistants, as of August 1998. Facilities now consist of a medical office on the White House's ground floor and a clinic in the Old Executive Office Building.

8

In Charge

As Boone looked back forty years to his birth in 1889, growing up in rural Pennsylvania, memories of his parents, the events beginning in 1929 were so different he vowed he could not have imagined them. Even after he went to medical school and joined the navy, it would never had crossed his mind that he could attain the remarkable post in which he now found himself. As he matured from a shy small-town boy, member of the Society of Friends, to a war hero and nationally recognized physician he gained self-confidence. His closeness to three presidents did not bring him to feel that he himself was important. He felt that he had occupied positions where he could help with the nation's work and currently was himself physician to the president. If a president during the 1920s, or members of his family felt ill, Boone was at hand.

He looked forward to working with the Hoovers, who were so easy to deal with. To Boone the president seemed a bit formal, to be sure, but not difficult, and there was no fear he was dealing with a brusque, remote personage, but instead a friend—in both senses, personal as well as religious. The Hoover years were to be the best of Boone's White House experiences.

1

Now that Boone had become physician to the White House after seven frustrating years in the number-two post, how did he set out to make his mark? His first task was to assess the physical well-being and health needs of his principal patient—President Hoover. Boone wondered how any man could possess the stamina to achieve what Hoover had done as an engineer, as protector to the Belgian people when threatened with starvation during the world war, as head of the wartime food administration, as provider of food to postwar Europe, and as secretary of commerce under Harding and Coolidge.

The opportunities Boone had to become acquainted with Hoover and observe his work at the commerce department and particularly the assignment to care for him during the visit to South America provided a starting point. Boone recognized Hoover's retentive memory, ability to converse on virtually any subject, his working long hours with little time for eating, sleep, or exercise. Writing to an uncle, he observed that "his is the greatest mind with which I have ever come in contact. He is the most indefatigable worker I have known."[1]

Boone noted Hoover's smoking cigars and pipes, but there is no evidence he tried to discourage the smoking, probably because the effects were not nearly as well-known as they are today. Boone was amused and amazed by how the president demonstrated sleight of hand when, after accepting a gift cigar, he stealthily transferred it to his pocket in exchange for one of the strong cigars made especially for him.

Boone had taken the first step in dealing with Hoover's lack of exercise by introducing him to medicine ball during the voyage aboard the *Utah*. Yet he lacked detailed knowledge of the president's physical condition. Mindful of his frustration over failure to convince General Sawyer of the importance of subjecting President Harding to a full physical examination and afterward the speculation about whether such an examination might have lengthened Harding's life, Boone resolved that things would be different now.

The very next day after President Hoover's inauguration, Boone told him of the need to examine his physical condition so as to establish a norm or benchmark against which to measure variances. Boone quoted a sentence from a speech Hoover had made: "Strong men must be on alert against insidious disease." This impressed the president. Hoover received only six days of grace before his physician insisted upon the examination—on Sunday so as not to interfere with work. Looking after his own health was not a priority with Hoover. Extracts from Boone's report of the examination follow:

On Sunday, March 10, I conducted a physical examination of President Hoover in his dressing room. He showed a great deal of interest in the examination... and asked many... good questions. Much to my amazement, he told me that he had never had his blood pressure taken theretofore.

I found him in very good physical condition, except that his pulse was not as strong as I would have expected in a man of his physical proportions; and he showed dyspnea [or breathlessness] upon exertion of two minutes duration. His blood pressure was 120 over 70. Heart action was perfectly normal. Measurements were normal as well. Chest was clear. He had 3-inch expansion. Abdomen was negative. Too much avoirdupois. His circumference was 43 inches. His ears required removal of cerumen, he claiming that he collected it quite rapidly. Nose and throat were negative.

I told him that he would need to have eyes refracted. A man of his years [55] no doubt required glasses, with the amount of reading that he was compelled to do. Visible evidence that he needed considerable dental treatment. He said that he had been too busy for the last few years to give but very sketchy attention to his teeth. I told him that we needed to have X-rays of his mouth and also his chest and I wished to have an electrocardiographic tracing made... Upon this examination his skin was negative, which was not subsequently the case... His weight stripped was 190 pounds, which I knew was much too much for him. I told him I would like him to get down to 175 and not above 180 pounds.[2]

When it came to dentistry, the president at first insisted on visiting the civilian dentist who had treated him for years, rather than having a navy dentist come to the White House, as Boone preferred. After receiving a bill that both Boone and Hoover considered exorbitant, he agreed to using the navy's dentists. Incidentally, Boone protested the $100 and succeeded in cutting it in half.

As a follow-up Boone had a discussion with the president about the need for exercise. The president was known to be an avid fisherman and loved to watch baseball games. These were excellent diversions but offered little more. Hoover loathed horseback riding so much—as a result of having been forced to ride as an engineer abroad—that he ordered the horses reserved for White House use returned to the Fort Myer stables.

When told by Hoover that he had engaged a masseur regularly, Boone said that what was needed was active outdoor exercise, not the passive type represented by a massage. He had known of cases in which rubdowns of hypertensive people brought complications. Moreover, he did not want anyone such as a masseur, not under his direct control, involved in the president's health.

Hoover's sole personal exercise had been setting-up exercises, used as a relief from sitting day after day in a train or a steamer stateroom during a lifetime of travel. Boone felt that this exercise did not meet the president's needs.

The White House physician was hounded by reporters who wanted to know how he intended to keep Hoover fit. He said he would welcome suggestions, and he received a flood of them: swimming, bowling, lawnbowling, handball, punching bag, archery, volleyball, woodworking, horseshoes, ladder climbing, rowing machine. Some bizarre pieces of equipment offered by manufacturers included: the Battlecreek Health Horse used by President Coolidge, the Simplex Spine Adjuster that claimed "if used daily mornings and evenings, will absolutely prevent any and all diseases, and with judicious use, will restore to health most diseases," the Vibrall Chair that "vibrates at the rate of 300 times per minute and gives one the sensation of riding horseback," the Sun-Bask Electric Cabinet, and the Miracle Health Builder. A well-meaning Connecticut "doctor" wrote: "I define exercise, find the circulation to be the key, reject muscle training (work!) and develop physiological use of the chest (aspiration of the thorax)."[3]

Boone decided to try out his own idea. He asked the president if he would be willing to play medicine ball as he had done on board the *Utah*. The answer was not encouraging. Hoover said his day was too full to allow exercise. The only time he could possibly devote to it would be in the morning before breakfast, and he did not think anyone would be willing to join him at that hour. He added, with all due respect, that passing the ball back and forth with Boone would become terribly boring.

The doctor persisted, saying he thought he could find people to join him in exercise if Hoover would give him a list of those he would like to invite. A day or two later Hoover handed Boone a list. It included Associate Justice Harlan F. Stone of the Supreme Court; Secretary of the Interior Ray Lyman Wilbur (himself a physician); Attorney General Mitchell; Postmaster General Walter Brown; Secretary of Agriculture Arthur Hyde; Secretary of the Treasury Ogden Mills; Assistant Secretary of War Patrick J. Hurley; Assistant Secretary of the Navy Ernest Jahncke; Mark Sullivan, the prominent journalist; William Hard, the commentator and writer; and the president's principal secretary, Larry Richey.

Boone interviewed each man, challenging him to contribute to the president's health by exercising on the White House lawn. He gave physical examinations to those who consented. Candidates declined, offering excuses: Mills did not like to get up early; Hyde had some kind of disability, didn't think he was strong enough; Brown said his labors as postmaster general made him tired. Hurley tried to participate despite a bad medical history, and for him the exercise proved too strenuous. Mitchell said he did not think it right to throw a heavy ball at the president of the United States, but Boone convinced him it was a favor rather than an insult.

After he had lined up the participants Boone dreamed up a game that refined and made more interesting the one played on the *Utah*. He marked out a thirty-by-sixty-foot court alongside the fountain on the White House south lawn and raised a net to nine feet suspended between poles. A medicine ball weighing from six to eight pounds completed the equipment, with the six-pounder proving most popular. Rules were established, including scoring as in tennis.

The first game was played at 7:10 A.M., April 8. Participants were Hoover, Stone, Wilbur, Hyde, Richey, and Boone. Later the group expanded, leading to designation by the press as the Medicine Ball Cabinet. "The game was slower than it later developed because of the small number of participants," Boone remembered. "We were not as agile or experienced in the game as we were later on. It was wise it was slower...I wanted to make sure...that the President...would not have to jump around too fast, play too violently early in our exercise program."⁴

The game gathered steam. *The Philadelphia Inquirer* reporter Thomas F. Healey wrote of Hoover's participation that "while someone is lunging that 6-pound sphere at him, if he doesn't keep his eye and his mind on the ball he may be socked in the midriff or be 'taken,' as the Englishman says, 'with a hard one in the nose.'"⁵ Boone noted that the president many times got socked with the ball. There was no respect of persons. Justice Stone was a powerful man, a former All-American guard at Columbia University. He could throw that ball with terrific force. Boone said he had seen players spun around when they caught a ball from Stone.

A regular routine was established, beginning with Boone's arrival at 6:30 when he would chat with the president as he shaved and dressed. By 7:10 members of the Medicine Ball Cabinet had gathered on the lawn or called in with excuses. Then the rough and tumble began, no holds barred. After a half hour the group gathered under a magnolia tree for juice and coffee.

With no regard for rain, snow, or sleet, the game was played day in, day out, except Sundays, during the four years of the administration. Boone acknowledged that during the winter months it was barely dawn at the 7:10 starting time, which made it difficult to see the ball, especially if it was foggy.

June 19, 1932, three years after medicine ball was introduced to the White House, a *Washington Sunday Star* magazine article had this to say about the game: "Last fall, when the members of the...football team which Herbert Hoover served as business manager [in his college days]...visited the White House, he invited them to join the medicine ball session. They did, but quite a number didn't like it, and some dropped out. Too strenuous for gentlemen in their fifties!"⁶

Members of the press expressed concern that the game was arduous and undignified. But before long, as Hoover lost weight and his physical condition improved, they changed their tune. As Healey of the *Inquirer* wrote, "There is a decided psychological effect, which is as necessary to the good health of the president as the physical effect. There is, of course, the decided benefit of the exercise, the fresh air, the fun of the thing, the hearty appetite that follows. But more important, perhaps, is the fact that during that half-hour of strenuous effort Mr. Hoover forgets he is President of the United States."[7] Healey went on to say: "This young doctor, whose boyhood was spent in Pottsville, Pennsylvania, and who received his medical education in Philadelphia, has a big job on his hands. He is competent. The president is safe in his hands because Dr. Boone possesses the scientific skill and the . . . common sense to take good care of the health of the nation's chief."[8]

Each of the players, even those who entered the game begrudgingly, said to Boone at one time or another, "I feel like a new man," or something similar.

Boone knew of no other such consistent on-schedule exercise by any president of the United States. He was quoted in one article as saying, "I consider the president's medicine ball cabinet definite proof that heart muscles, and indeed, all the body musculature, can be developed to meet consistently heavy physical demands even after the age of 50—if it is done with proper guidance and discretion, and guardedly."[9]

In the final days of the Hoover administration, as the president and his cabinet prepared to separate, the medicine ball received recognition for its contribution to camaraderie and health. Sixteen balls were signed by the players as memorabilia. At a dinner hosted by Justice and Mrs. Stone, Helen Boone read a poem she composed, an extract of which is quoted below:

> He was the White House Doctor,
> And he stoppeth one of three,
> A Justice of the Supreme Court,
> Who was on his way to tea.
>
> "What wantest thou?" the Justice said,
> With a glitter in his eye.
> "To join the President's Medicine Ball,
> Before the sun is high."
>
> "But I've not thrown a medicine ball

Since I was twenty-four.
And now I'm in my sixties,
I'll exercise no more." . . .

We'll miss our morning exercise
And the comradeship it brought.
We'll ne'er forget the happy hours.
We'll give them many a thought.

A Toast, to our Beloved Chief
And to his Ladye fair—
"Luck, happiness and health supreme,"
We hope you both may share.

With apologies to

Samuel Taylor Coleridge [10]

With Hoover's departure from the White House, medicine ball was forgotten for fifty-five years. In 1988, in celebration of the thirty-first president's 114th birthday in West Branch, Iowa, it was revived under the name of "Hoover-ball," with teams competing in a tournament and press coverage by *Sports Illustrated*. Hoover's grandson, Herbert C. ("Pete") Hoover III, and Boone's grandson, Milton F. (Mickey) Heller III, participated in the Iowa games that have become annual events in conjunction with celebration of Hoover's birthday.

A step toward returning Hoover-ball to the south lawn was taken in 1990 with a tournament on Washington's Mall, with Sen. Mark Hatfield of Oregon as a participant.

Another Boone innovation for Hoover was to set aside at least a half hour each day for an early-evening nap. Naps proved helpful in alleviating fatigue, permitting the president to lead conversation at dinner and to work into the night. Incidentally, it was the Hoovers' practice to entertain guests daily at all three meals.

As the president gained confidence in Boone, he tried to become a cooperative patient. He began to watch his diet, especially rich foods. He would make time for dental treatment, badly needed after years of neglect. He avoided contact with people who had colds. He gave up the routine of shaking hands at noon each day with visitors, a practice followed by presidents since virtually the beginning of the presidency. During the Harding and Coolidge presidencies, long lines of Washington visitors had formed outside the executive offices as the noon hour approached, and people would pass through the offices and the president would shake hands for whatever value the shaking (perhaps like the royal touch of French monarchs in the eighteenth century and earlier) possessed.

In retrospect, the combination of what must have been good genes, a cooperative patient, and a dedicated, single-minded physician paid off: Hoover lived to age ninety, a record exceeded by no other president and equaled only by John Adams.

2

One of Boone's patients during the Hoover years was Marie Curie, who from a poor Polish governess in France had become a scientist and worked with her husband, Pierre, to discover radium, thereby achieving fame. Having won two Nobel prizes, she was in Washington in 1929 to receive honors from President Hoover at the National Academy of Sciences.

Boone was asked to see Madame Curie professionally, and although we do not know the nature of the diagnosis or treatment, he had this to say: "A very sweet older lady. Her hands were very disfigured from radium burns. She had a sad expression and was dressed plainly in a long, black silk dress. She reminded me of the painting of `Whistler's Mother.'"[11] Noting her retiring nature, he quoted Albert Einstein as having said, "Marie Curie is, of all celebrated beings, the only one whom fame has not corrupted."[12] Boone was thrilled when a few days afterward he received an autographed photograph and a note: "My dear Dr. Boone: I want to thank you for your care of me when I was in the White House. I felt very safe under your protection. Sincerely yours, M. Curie."[13]

Thomas A. Edison was among patients from outside the Washington scene treated by Boone during the Hoover administration. When Henry Ford staged a grand celebration in 1929 in the Detroit area in honor of Edison, who had invented the incandescent light just fifty years earlier, Boone was there with President and Mrs. Hoover. During dinner speeches Mrs. Hoover, seated to the right of Edison, recognized that the inventor was not feeling well, so she summoned Boone with a wiggle of her finger and asked him to take a seat behind Edison. Soon Edison asked Mrs. Hoover to be excused and was led on Boone's arm through heavy curtains into the lobby. On the way out the deaf gentleman exclaimed in a loud voice, "I hate those damn things! They bore the hell out of me."[14] Boone determined that the inventor was suffering from fatigue, arranged for him to rest until dinner was over, took him home and put him to bed, and turned the case over to his family doctor. Several years later a newspaper published a story about the incident, based on an Associated Press dispatch, under the caption, "Hoover's Doctor Saved Edison's Life in Detroit."[15] According to Boone, the caption and article were highly exaggerated.

To the doctor each patient was important regardless of station. No society doctor, he treated each the same.

Mrs. Hoover enjoyed good health—certainly better than Mrs. Harding's—but was such a busy person and so caught up in activities of her husband that her health could suffer. Boone said he did not know any couple who shared their lives so completely, that Mrs. Hoover was of tremendous assistance to her husband, sharing problems and offering counsel but without interfering. Being sensitive, she felt the stabs of political life more keenly than he, in Boone's view.

Allan Hoover was not among Boone's more cooperative patients. Twenty-one at the time of his father's inauguration, he resisted treatment and asked that Boone justify his recommendations. Boone felt that Mrs. Hoover overindulged her younger son and gave in to him. But the president had told Boone he must be the one to enforce orders and apply whatever restrictions on Allan were necessary. The father went so far as to send Boone to the Harvard Business School, where Allan was enrolled, to check on his son's health and to confer with one of his teachers, Gen. Georges F. Doriot, presumably about

Allan's studies. While Boone relished medicine, he found the policeman aspect of the job distasteful.

Of all medical matters Boone handled during the Hoover administration, Allan's older brother, Herbert, Jr., was the most difficult, from both a medical standpoint and the strain imposed on the president's physician. In the autumn of 1930, just as Boone was beginning to feel burned out, he feared he faced a repetition of the tragedy that befell Calvin Coolidge, Jr.

When Herbert Jr., a radio engineer, arrived from California in September, the president noted that his son looked underweight and was tired. He asked Boone to examine the six-foot Herbert, who had lost twenty pounds over five months. The examination included chest X rays at the naval hospital. When Boone assembled his own findings together with the radiologist's report he was shocked. Tubercular infection of the lungs was a possibility. One must remember that in those days tuberculosis, or "consumption," as it once had been known, was both life-threatening and far more prevalent than today.

Boone told the president he was suspicious but not at all certain that young Herbert was tubercular. He recommended consultation. To avoid publicity Boone suggested the consultant should come from outside Washington. Boone went so far as to use a fictitious patient's name when telephoning the consultant to ask that they meet with the patient at Boone's apartment rather than at the White House. Dr. Louis Hamman, who had been chief of tuberculosis work at Johns Hopkins, duly arrived. He said he did not wish to learn of X ray findings until after he examined Herbert's chest. Upon completion of the examination Hamman said to Boone, "I am sorry, but I can't agree with you that there are any suspicious findings. Let's go to the naval hospital and review the X rays." After only a few moments of looking, Hamman threw his hands up in the air, pointed at a small cottonlike area in the right apex with rays extending from it down through parenchyma of the right lung, and exclaimed, "There is absolutely no question that this is a tubercular infection."[16]

Hamman returned to Baltimore, and Boone faced the task of breaking the news to the president. Finding Hoover alone in the second-floor office of the White House, he described the examination and the subsequent discussion of Hamman and Boone with the radiologist at the naval hospital, Dr. Spalding. With trepidation Boone told of the conclusions reached by all three physicians.

"The president turned very white, put his elbows on the desk and dropped his head into his hands," Boone reported. "He sat there for some minutes in dead silence."

Knowing Hoover, Boone anticipated the first question: "What are you going to do about it?"[17] He had outlined in his own mind a plan of care and therapy, assuming he would have responsibility for the case. Boone described a several-month regimen of rest, diet, and isolation. The president left the office to give his wife the bad news.

The question arose of notifying Herbert's wife, Peggy. Even before a phone call to California, Boone said to President and Mrs. Hoover, "I absolutely would oppose the children of Herbert and Mrs. Hoover, Jr., coming to the White House to be with their father. They positively must not be exposed to tubercular infection from him."[18] Peggy Hoover was insistent that the children accompany her. Boone prevailed, but little did he realize what distress his attitude would bring—not that it would have changed his stance. Boone was also anxious to limit contact by President and Mrs. Hoover and arranged for the patient to be moved, along with George Fox, to the president's camp on the Rapidan in Virginia.

With the diagnosis confirmed, the Hoovers directed Boone to release to the press information concerning the illness. Boone was quoted in a dispatch of September 23, 1930, as having said, "The inheritance of vigor that has served his father well throughout a strenuous life is expected to aid Herbert Hoover, Jr., in his fight against tuberculosis."[19] The forthright manner in which President and Mrs. Hoover dealt with the matter generated much favorable comment, illustrated by an Associated Press article: "The public announcement that President Hoover's son is under treatment for tuberculosis was commended today by health authorities who believe it will result in a wider play for science's most effective weapon against the dis-

ease—early diagnosis."[20] Boone counted editorials in 148 newspapers commenting favorably on the statement he issued. Only
two, the *Sioux City Tribune* and *Richmond Times Dispatch*, were
critical. The *Tribune* editorialized that "somebody has been
guilty of questionable taste," and went on to say: "It was of
doubtful necessity, in a case of that kind, to inform the young
man of the nature of his illness. The knowledge will be injurious
to him rather than beneficial."[21] The *Times Dispatch* felt that the
president's son's affairs were "none of the business of the American people."[22]

Ever since the public was so badly misled concerning the
health of President Roosevelt at the time of his campaign for a
fourth term in 1944, disclosure of illness in the White House has
been a warm topic. In long retrospect it seems that Boone acted
with remarkable correctness, diagnosing the affliction of the
president's son, bringing in a consultant, informing the president and following that task by a press release. His was a model
of White House medicine. As years passed, not only the Roosevelt case but also the later illness—a very serious heart
attack—of Pres. Dwight D. Eisenhower displayed how illnesses
should not be handled. (The Eisenhower case was more serious
than announced.) In contrast, the way in which Boone's good
sense took over and in due course made public knowledge of a
White House illness elicits admiration.

The illness of the Hoover son, a young man of twenty-seven,
turned out all right, albeit not without awkwardness between
Boone and the parents. While at the Rapidan and later in
Asheville, the patient improved. Neither Herbert nor his wife
and parents seemed to understand that tuberculosis could not be
cured within a short time in those days before antibiotics. They
became impatient with the slowness of recovery. Their desire to
return family life to normal became a source of frustration. Having nettled Herbert's wife by preventing her from bringing the
children to the White House, Boone felt compelled to continue to
protect the youngsters from infection from their father. When it
was proposed that they visit Herbert in Asheville, he again was
obliged to say no.

President Hoover wanted his physician to arrange for Herbert to come from Asheville for Christmas. Herbert's wife was there with the three children. Boone attempted to convince Hoover that Herbert's presence would be inimical to his own welfare and dangerous to others, especially the children. He was sure the president would understand.

Looking at Boone, the president asked, "Are you adamant in that opinion?"

"Mr. President, I cannot compromise my professional opinion."

Boone tells us that uncharacteristically "the president flushed and really stormed out of his dressing room into his bedroom, shutting the door, without having bid me 'goodnight'."[23] With a troubled heart, the physician returned to his apartment to tell his wife that their White House days were surely at an end.

In April 1931, Herbert came from Asheville for a brief stay. He went on to California, where Boone kept in touch as he continued his recovery.

9

The Hoover Administration

Fortunately for Boone, the stressful conditions under which he
worked during the illness and recovery of Herbert Hoover, Jr.,
were not typical of his service as physician to the White House
during the four years of the Hoover administration. Boone developed a close relationship with President and Mrs. Hoover,
for he was with the president day in, day out, on all but the
most formal occasions wearing the same kind of clothes as
Hoover—cutaway, silk hat, dinner jacket, sports or street
clothes; where formality was appropriate, Boone wore his uniform complete with railroad trousers, fore-and-aft hat,
epaulets, sword, and medals.

A schedule that demanded continuing attendance on the
president meant little time with Helen or Suzanne, who escaped
Washington's heat by spending summers in Swampscott as
guests of the Stearnses.

1

One form of recreation President Hoover did not enjoy was
sailing on the *Mayflower*. Boone recalled that whenever Hoover
came aboard during his service as secretary of commerce he
would bring a stack of paperwork and confine himself to his
cabin. It came as no surprise when he ordered the *Mayflower*
decommissioned. Boone was glad he was unable to be present
when the presidential flag was hauled down for the last time
June 7, 1929. His feelings were understandable. It was as the
ship's medical officer that he had been introduced to the White
House, and the seven years he had served aboard exceeded those

of any other officer for the twenty-seven years the ship had been in naval service.

As a footnote, it should be stated that *Mayflower*'s termination as the presidential yacht in 1929 did not end its life, for it lived at least nineteen years longer, surviving two fires and a sinking, serving in the Coast Guard in World War II, and sailing under various names in private ownership. It was last mentioned in the press in 1948, when as the steamship *Mala* it carried Jewish refugees from Europe to Haifa.

Retirement of the *Mayflower*, originally a 320-foot steel-hulled brigantine, did not mean Hoover had abandoned water transportation. With Boone and others he sailed to Puerto Rico in 1931 on board the battleship *Arizona*, sunk ten years later at Pearl Harbor and now a memorial. In October of the same year he took the battleship *Arkansas* from Annapolis to Yorktown to lead the sesquicentennial celebration of the Revolutionary War victory there. For fishing trips or entertaining such dignitaries as the queen of Siam, Hoover used the Department of Commerce's 105-foot cabin cruiser, the *Sequoia*. President Roosevelt and some of his successors would use *Sequoia* but it was hardly in the same class as the grand *Mayflower* that had brought so much pleasure to Presidents Theodore Roosevelt, Taft, Wilson, Harding, and Coolidge.

Since trout fishing was Hoover's favorite relaxation, he wasted no time looking for a retreat in a wooded area close to streams, at an elevation offering relief from summer heat, within a few hours from Washington. Just such a place was on the Rapidan River in the heart of what was to become Shenandoah National Park. Hoover personally paid the State of Virginia $25,000 for 160 acres and arranged to build a rustic camp, with the intention of turning it over to the Park Service upon retirement. Facilities consisted of khaki-colored tents, soon replaced by plain board buildings constructed by marines from a nearby camp. Rapidan Camp, as it became known, served as a weekend retreat as well as a place for conferences and entertaining such guests as British prime minister Ramsay MacDonald, together with Lindbergh and many others. Boone, of course, was always there with the president, and Helen and Suzanne often accompanied him, taking pleasure in riding along the mountain trails.

Rapidan Camp was a busy place. During that summer of 1929 there were walks, roads, and dams to be built, and the president made clear he expected guests as well as such staff members as Boone and Richey to pitch in. Boone reported that those participating in the daily medicine ball game at the White House had a fine opportunity to improve their performance by lifting and carrying heavy rocks. This was no rich man's playground. Boone was delighted when Friday or Saturday came and he could head for the Rapidan. Much of the time was spent just relaxing, reading, or working on jigsaw puzzles, but then there was horseshoe pitching, playing catch, fishing, hiking, and riding. Mrs. Hoover loved to ride up the streams and over the mountains, and Boone often accompanied her or served as a guide for guests.

One memorable ride took him to a tumble-down farmhouse and a tousle-haired boy, Ray Buraker, in jeans and torn shirt lolling on a split-rail fence. The encounter led Boone to tell the president about the shy eight- or nine-year-old boy and his impoverished family. Hoover seemed to identify with the lad, perhaps because he himself, as a youthful orphan had been sent with two nickels and a suit of clothes from his birthplace in Iowa to live with a poor uncle in Oregon.

The president asked Boone to offer Ray five dollars if he would bring a live possum the next time he visited the camp. A couple of weeks later Ray showed up with the possum in a sack, Boone introduced him to the president, and Hoover paid the fee. Boone saw to it that Ray met the Lindberghs, guests of the Hoovers. It was either the president or Mrs. Hoover—Boone could not remember—who said to Ray, "I am sure that you are pleased to meet Colonel Lindbergh," conveying the message that he was a lucky boy to meet this man whom the world had acclaimed a hero. The boy said, "I never heared of him." At that point, Lindbergh left the group, disappearing behind a large tree, and Boone followed him. With an embarrassed look the flier said, "That is one of the most consoling things that I have heard since I have made my flight. I am so gratified to find somebody who never 'heared' of me."[1] He went on to tell Boone how he had become so imprisoned by adulation that he could no longer wear anything like a hat, watch chain, or necktie without having some admirer take it.

The most important consequence of Boone's chance meeting with Ray Buraker in that mountain clearing was that it led the Hoovers to pay for construction of a schoolhouse near the camp and engage a teacher, making possible the schooling of thirty children who otherwise would have been deprived of education. The only school was miles away.

The first fishing trip of Boone's life, in the company of Hoover, Wilbur, and Richey, was unforgettable. The president was an accomplished fly fisherman and had written a book on this avocation. It was in June of 1929 at Richey's place near Catoctin Furnace, north of Frederick, Maryland, that the four began the day by going their separate ways along the cascading mountain stream and beautiful still pools. At the end of the day the fishermen gathered to compare catches. Hoover declared that Wilbur took the honors. Almost as an afterthought the president spotted his physician standing shyly in the background and asked, "Boone, did you catch anything?"

"Yes," replied Boone.

"Where are your trout?"

"In my creel, sir."

"Lay them out on the table so we can all see them."

Hoover laid Boone's largest trout alongside Wilbur's and exclaimed, "Why, Ray, you did not win the prize. Boone won it. He's got the largest trout." Fastening his eyes on Boone, the president asked, "What kind of fly did you catch that trout on?"

Boone said, "Fly?"

"Yes, fly."

"I did not catch it on a fly."

"You didn't catch it on a fly? Just what did you catch it on?"

"A worm."

"Worm!" the president exclaimed with derision. "The first rule in fishing expeditions: we *never* fish with *worms*."[2]

Boone counted friendship with the Hoovers as the most

gratifying aspect of his work at the White House. Christmas Eve, 1929, the Hoovers' first in the White House, Suzanne sat among thirty dinner guests at the president's right. She recalled how the president made it a practice to converse with children as though they were adults, never talking down to them. He always seemed to have a wire puzzle in his pocket and loved to slip a morsel to a dog under the table.

Suzanne had the run of the White House, and her parents were guests there on virtually all occasions. The ties by no means ended when the Hoovers left the White House. Just as the Boones kept in touch with Mrs. Coolidge until her death, so they remained friends with the Hoovers. When in the late 1930s Suzanne came to Palo Alto to visit her beau, a Stanford student, it was Mrs. Hoover who bailed out the carless couple by lending them her shiny Ford V-8 coupe. In June 1941, when Suzanne was to marry that same beau (this writer), the Hoovers sent a telegram stating that it was only celebration of Stanford's Fiftieth Anniversary that prevented them from being present. One of the most prized possessions of the Boones' youngest grandchild, Dr. Joel Boone Heller, is a letter from Hoover to Suzanne congratulating mother and child when young Joel was born on October 8, 1961, three years before former president Hoover died at the age of ninety.

Among the many notables with whom Boone developed an acquaintance during the Hoover years was Marshal Henri Pétain, France's most distinguished soldier. Pétain came to the United States in October, 1931, to represent France at the Yorktown sesquicentennial. One morning as Pétain emerged from his room at the White House he stopped Boone in the hall to interrogate him about his medals, which Pétain had observed while the physician had been in Yorktown. Fingering the ribbons, Pétain had noted the Croix de Guerre with Two Palms. He said in French, "Where is your Légion d'honneur?"[3]

Embarrassed, Boone indicated he had not been honored by such a high award.

The marshal quizzed Boone about participation in battles on French soil during the Great War, he turned to an aide, and said something Boone could not understand. Months later Boone received in the mail the Légion d'honneur of the officer class, accompanied by a scroll citation signed: "M. Pétain." He turned the medal over to the State Department pending authorization by Congress of acceptance. It was not until the Eisenhower administration that he was able to accept.

Another Frenchman with whom he became acquainted was Premier Pierre Laval. Boone had been called on to escort Laval to a conference and described Laval as a courteous gentleman.

Based on experiences in France during the war the physician had come to regard Pétain as "France's great soldier-leader." Yet within ten years these two Frenchmen were destined to become Nazi puppets in the Vichy government of France, followed by Laval's execution and Pétain's exile.

At this time a war acquaintance and friend, John Balch—a hospital corpsman who had won the Medal of Honor in France—came back into Boone's life. In response to a telephone call to the White House, Balch was invited to the Boone apartment, where the physician was shocked to see that the handsome, well-groomed youth he had known appeared a disheveled, unshaven tramp. After the war Balch had married and done well in the haberdashery business until the depression wiped him out. At the urging of other veterans he had joined the Bonus March to Washington. Boone abhorred the idea of a march against the government. He convinced Balch to accept his hospitality and clean up his act both literally and figuratively. Boone devoted a great deal of time and effort to finding employment for Balch, first with the government and later with the Republican national committee in Chicago, where he was able to resume a business career. This was yet another example of how Boone throughout his life went out of his way to assist friends.

Boone seemed to have a knack for identifying talent in diverse fields. One example was Arthur S. Prettyman, a mess attendant at the time he met him on the *Maryland* carrying President-elect and Mrs. Hoover to South America. Boone recognized an outstanding individual and took steps for his transfer to the *Mayflower* and then to the White House, where Prettyman served part-time as Boone's chauffeur. Prettyman became President Roosevelt's valet and was with Roosevelt when he died in Warm Springs in 1945.

2

The years with the Hoovers passed, and before Boone could realize it, it was time for the presidential election in 1932, during which the sitting president, Hoover, faced an enormous challenge from his Democratic contender, Roosevelt. On Boone's part, and of course privately, there was no question where his sympathies lay. He had admired Hoover more than his two interesting and in many ways agreeable predecessors. Privately Boone was a political conservative and drawn to the Republican Party. He hoped for Hoover's reelection.

It was with anguish that Boone watched the almost catastrophic decline in Hoover's political fortunes as the Great Depression, which opened with the break in the stock market in October 1929, moved uncertainly for a while and eventually turned everything downward, making the political chances of an incumbent president impossible. The president of 1929–33 of course knew that reelection might not be part of his political life but did the best he could in public to show he was not intimidated by his opponent. Privately Hoover was not at all confident. In the midst of the campaign in 1932 he exclaimed in a tired moment to Boone, "I don't see why anyone would want this damnable job."[4]

Boone remembered a notable occasion at the Rapidan when Hoover's confidence was at very low ebb and the president, who otherwise would have shown hopefulness, perhaps confidence, made no effort to disguise his dejection. Hoover's supporters had gone to lengths to invite twenty-three newspapermen and photographers to the Rapidan for an "intimate get-together." They had arranged for the president to ride a horse—not Hoover's favorite occupation. Hoover looked bored and indeed acted ungraciously that day. As Boone noted, the president's mind was so much on other things, especially the country's economic condition, which nothing seemed capable of turning around. On this awful day at the Rapidan the Republican president put on puttees to show that he was a hail fellow but perhaps purposely placed them wrongly, each on the wrong leg.

Hoover's feelings often burst forth in unexpected ways. When in the company of Edison, the president vented his wrath with the newspaper photographers and their ever-present lights. Well within the hearing of Boone he said to Edison, "Why did you invent the damn things?"[5]

Not long before the election, when Boone visited his wartime comrade Dick Derby, Dick's wife, Ethel, and Ethel's mother, Mrs. Theodore Roosevelt, he was delighted to learn that these Roosevelts were solidly behind President Hoover, even though Franklin Roosevelt's wife, Eleanor, was a niece of Theodore Roosevelt. Derby went so far as to say, "Franklin D. Roosevelt is and always has been vacillating, unreliable, unsound, veneer of charm and personality without mental . . . ability."[6] In a thank-you note to the Derbys, Boone proclaimed, "We as a nation need President Hoover!"[7]

More of an optimist than realist, Boone held to the belief that Hoover would be reelected, despite the pounding his hero was taking from Roosevelt and his supporters. Even election night, with the Hoovers and intimate friends at the Hoover home in Palo Alto, Boone expected to be a "gala social evening." It was only when, in the middle of dinner, the president received a note from his valet, excused himself from the table, and failed to return that Boone became alarmed. After dinner Boone and six close friends joined the president in his study, where they learned that the note had informed Hoover that early in the evening voters in New York State had gone for Roosevelt. Hoover knew he had been defeated.

Returning to Washington by train, Boone could not help but draw a parallel with the trip he had made in August 1923 on board President Harding's funeral train: "That was a trip of deep sorrow and mourning, whereas those of us traveling with the president [Hoover] were deeply disappointed that he had not been re-elected."[8]

For Boone there followed a period of uncertainty. After the defeat of Hoover, the consummate nonpolitican, by the wily

151

Governor Roosevelt, Boone had cause to question whether he would be retained as presidential physician. To an observer it would have been clear that he had thrown his lot in with Hoover when he spoke about the president's fitness for continuing in office. Boone regarded himself as a navy officer and physician—above politics—but at the same time was intensely loyal to his patient, Hoover. He was soon to find that he could not have it both ways.

Two weeks after the election, a prominent Washington lawyer, Houston Thompson, an intimate of Franklin Roosevelt, offered to intervene in the interest of having the president-elect appoint Boone, but Boone discouraged such activity, declaring he was weary. At about the same time Boone did give consideration to a "high position," not otherwise identified, at Princeton University, offered by the board of trustees. Although the offer was attractive, he reached the same conclusion as in 1924 when Will Hays, George Eastman, and the director general of the American College of Surgeons, Edward Martin, encouraged him to organize a program at medical schools and other institutions through the medium of motion pictures. Boone decided that the satisfaction of continuing in the service of his country as a navy physician was greater.

In the waning days of the administration the Boones remained visible among guests at social functions. The season closed with a White House reception for 1,700 guests on February 25, 1933. Children of administration members were singled out for attention at the request of Mrs. Hoover, and Suzanne, a thirteen-year-old carrying a nosegay made by Mrs. Hoover, attracted much attention. She "looked like a Dresden doll in a beautiful gown with a full skirt," according to Boone.[9] As her parents gazed at her, poised and dignified beyond her years, their hearts swelled with pride.

As Hoover dressed for dinner on the evening of March 3, his last as a resident of the White House, he spoke with Boone in a more intimate and sentimental manner than ever before, saying, "Doctor, ours has been a wonderful relationship. I can never express adequately my gratitude for what you have done for me and mine."

Boone responded, "I have viewed our relationship as a most sacred one."

To this the president said, "A relationship between a patient and a physician is a wonderful relationship, I have learned; but the relationship between a president and his physician is a sacred relationship, as you have just properly observed."[10]

Boone remarked that if Hoover were to come across a civil position suitable to Boone he would appreciate hearing of it.

The reply was, "You had better keep your 'anchorage' in these troublesome times, for we may have worse days ahead."

3

Boone met Governor Roosevelt after the election, on November 22, 1932, when the president-elect arrived at the White House for a conference: "I was shocked when I saw how crippled Governor Roosevelt was and with what painful difficulty he walked laboriously on metal crutches to the elevator, supported by a New York State trooper . . . Doubtless, the governor had full-length braces on his legs. His face was very lined and furrowed, both up and down and crossways. This amazed me. I had seen him many times and conferred with him when he was Assistant Secretary of the Navy . . . He was then a tall, erect, very handsome man with a pleasant smile and very affable manner."[11] Boone remembered well the reception that Roosevelt, as assistant secretary of the navy, had had for him at the time he pinned a Croix de Guerre on Boone following the Great War.

After leaving the conference with Hoover, Roosevelt encountered Boone in the hallway, and when Ike Hoover started to introduce the two Roosevelt interrupted cheerfully, "Hello, Joel Boone. How are you?" As the governor made his way to the car, the conversation continued. Two points impressed Boone: "He referred to his sunning himself a lot at Warm Springs, Georgia, and said he wanted me to see that place . . . He called back to say he would be seeing me frequently."[12]

Under a dateline of Warm Springs, November 30, an Associated Press dispatch related: "It is reported President-elect Roosevelt contemplates abolishing the post of personal physician to the President."[13] How could that be? Eight days earlier Roosevelt had led Boone to believe the two would be seeing each other "frequently"—presumably in a patient/physician relationship. To a layman it would seem that if ever a president needed a physician at hand it would be Roosevelt.

Thereafter Boone received mixed signals. On February 1, 1933, he received orders: "When directed by the President of the United States on or about 4 March, 1933, you will regard yourself detached from duty as Physician to the White House, etc."[14] Whether they reflected an attitude toward Boone in particular or were part of a general program to open the way for new appointments was unclear.

At a luncheon on inauguration day, Sara Delano Roosevelt, the president's mother, introduced to Boone, took him aside and said, "You give the very best care to my son. Keep a close watch over him. You know he has had a very long and a very serious illness. He needs the careful care and supervision of a physician."[15] Four days later the new president went out of his way to visit Boone in his office and clinic, commenting that the layout was "splendid and that he would find great use for it." He said to Boone, "It is grand to have you here, Doctor."[16]

During this perplexing first month of the Roosevelt administration, Boone's behavior was decorous. In contrast to the years when he had access to any part of the White House and visited the family quarters almost daily, he never entered any part of the building above the main floor. He had no social contact with any member of the household. He conducted no physical examination of the president. although he was prepared to do so if requested. Only twice did Roosevelt make reference to his own health—when he expressed a desire to have Boone accompany him to Warm Springs to see how polio cases were treated, later when he casually mentioned nasal trouble. Treatment of Mrs. Roosevelt for a sore finger was as close medically as Boone got to the first family.

The manner in which Boone learned what lay in store seems best described in his own words:

Thursday, March 29th, the president stopped by my office door . . . He stated that he wished to express his appreciation for my helpful and successful treatment of Mrs. Roosevelt, that the treatment she had had in New York had been unsuccessful, that he knew I was going to be able to afford her great relief and improvement, and that he hoped I would continue to treat her just as frequently as seemed necessary.

The next day at 4:30 in the afternoon, a colored messenger from the Navy Department brought a sealed envelope and stated, "Here is Dr. Boone's orders detaching him from the White House." The envelope contained a modification of my orders of February 1, with a pink "urgent" slip clipped to the corners. The orders stated that my orders of February 1 were so modified that I would consider myself detached as Physician to the White House as of March 30, 1933, [and that my next permanent duty would be as of Chief of the Medical Service of the hospital ship *Relief*, which as part of the U.S. Fleet was then in Pacific waters]. Because of the lateness of the hour it was impossible to comply with my orders that day, so I reported to the Surgeon General the next morning. . . .

The next day [presidential] Secretary McIntyre was informed of the receipt of these orders, and he remarked that the President had been giving consideration to the matter for several days and he came to the conclusion that he did not desire to have a personal physician, believing it was good politics not to have one. With this deduction, McIntyre said he was in accord and asked if I did not agree to the principle. I told him that there was no relation to the position of Physician to the White House with politics. He said he knew the president wanted to see me before I departed.

I reported to the Surgeon General of the Navy, Admiral Rossiter, who said that he was sorry that he had not called me up the day before to warn me of the action that had been taken, but that he was in a rush and that it had slipped his mind. He stated, as did Secretary McIntyre, that it was the wish that Fox (George A. Fox, Chief Pharmacist's Mate) be continued on duty at the White House and that the office be maintained as at present. I asked whether it was his desire that I should give Fox any instructions as to how to perform his duties and whom to summon in the event of an emergency. He said, "No," that he would contact him and there would be an officer designated to provide for the professional services of the White House. A little later he stated that Lieutenant Commander Ross McIntire had been directed to report to the White House the next day and to go there every morning for as long a period each day as necessary and then hold himself in readiness for White House calls.

I went to the Naval Hospital, congratulated Dr. McIntire on his detail and offered him every assistance within my power and volunteered to go to the White House the following day, show him about and make him familiar with the equipment and surroundings. He stated he had verbal orders on the telephone to perform this duty but that he should keep himself in the background, and while he did not know how his position would be interpreted, he meant to make a real job out of it. I apprised him of the statute enacted in April 1930, which provided for an ex-officio rank for the Army or Naval medical officer assigned as the Physician to the White House.

When I returned to the White House to see the president, as I was directed to do, he received me very cordially and, shaking hands, he said he regretted very much seeing me go as he had wished to have me stay with him, but that "they (without designating to whom 'they' referred) felt it was for the best interests of your career to have other duties at this time."

I returned later to meet Dr. McIntire in the offices of the Physician to the White House and he, Fox and I discussed the position in the way I performed my duties.[17]

So ended eleven years with four presidents as assistant White House physician to Harding and Coolidge, physician to Hoover, and for less than one month interim caretaker of the White House clinic. On March 31, Boone reported to the Naval Medical School for refresher courses in medicine, and two months later, after Suzanne graduated, the Boones were off to California preparatory to duty on the hospital ship *Relief*. They took an abundance of memories. More important, they carried with them treasured friendships with Mrs. Coolidge and John, with the Hoover family, and with hundreds of others in all walks of life.

10

After the White House

Serving as physician to the White House during the Hoover administration represented the high point of Boone's career, but by no means did it mean that he faded into obscurity. In the years that followed his departure from Washington in 1933, he continued to distinguish himself.

The immediate move from the sophistication of Washington to the depressed town of San Pedro, California, home port of the *Relief*, was much harder on Helen and Suzanne than on Joel, who could look forward to new and different professional challenges. The thirteen-year-old Suzanne found it difficult to make the transition from Washington's Potomac School, a private institution favored by cabinet members and foreign diplomats, to the rough-and-tumble atmosphere of San Pedro's public school, where the children of longshoremen predominated. On the first day, dressed in her "Eastern garb," she heard one classmate ask her in all seriousness, "Are you our new teacher?"[1]

Despite reduction in rank from navy captain to commander, the price of holding a temporary rank that went with the post of physician to the White House, Joel suffered a further pay cut, as did all service personnel during the Great Depression. Helen's financial management kept bread on the table and a roof overhead.

Boone spent the remainder of the 1930s up to World War II in billets with the navy and marines on the Pacific coast, responsible among other tasks for medical support for a new type of warfare—amphibious landings.

Escorting Suzanne to the altar

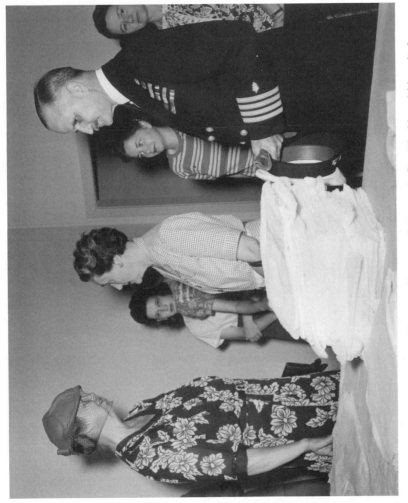

With wife, escorting Eleanor Roosevelt through Seattle Naval Hospital
(Official U.S. Navy Photograph)

1

The depression years came to an end with the imminence and then the reality of war in 1941; at once Boone's work took a new and serious turn. The Pacific coast bustled with construction of a new navy, a huge fleet that at war's end equaled all the other navies of the world combined. In this enterprise the months passed in a whirl, and Boone helped plan and then manage facilities for care on a massive scale of wounded returning from attacks upon the islands leading to Japan and then attacks on the home islands themselves.

As the war moved toward its end a new duty appeared. Boone was called to Washington to meet with the chief of naval operations, Adm. Ernest J. King, who informed him he was being ordered to a new position as Third Fleet medical officer on Admiral William F. Halsey's staff, with the rank of commodore. King told Boone that Halsey had opposed such a position and to let him know at any time if he became so frustrated he wished to be reassigned. Halsey was so leery of having this staff officer "interfere" in fleet activities he even tried to have him quartered on a ship other than the flagship *Missouri*. But "Bull" Halsey had met his match. Boone insisted on flying to Guam to confer with Adm. Chester W. Nimitz, commander-in-chief of the Pacific Fleet. Boone gained Nimitz's backing and succeeded in winning Halsey's confidence and friendship as well. His status as the second highest-ranking officer on a staff of sixty officers and two hundred men, junior only to Halsey's chief-of-staff, Adm. Carney, was acknowledged by his seating at meals to Halsey's left and by the ship captain's insistence that Boone occupy his cabin while he moved to a sea cabin on the bridge. Boone's progress in overcoming resistance to his position was evidenced in a letter he wrote on May 24, 1945, to Vice Adm. Ross T. McIntire, navy surgeon general and Boone's successor as physician to the White House: "It gives me inexpressible gratitude to present to you such a favorable report on the proper establishment of the Fleet Medical Officer's status. I am busy now, as an integral part of the staff of this Fleet. We are all working together harmoniously for the success of a common mission."[2]

With Halsey and his chief of staff, Carney, on deck of battleship *Missouri* (Official U.S. Naval Photograph)

Despite general acceptance, Boone did meet resistance in attempting to broaden his role. In another letter he wrote: "I had hoped to have put out to the THIRD Fleet components that the Fleet Medical Officer would have 'general supervision of medical activities of the THIRD Fleet but that administrative details would remain as at present'... My proposal to have sent out such a letter was disapproved."[3] Anyone who knew Boone realized he would not let the wording of a position description stand in his way. While another ship was either fueling or being fueled by the *Missouri* under way, he would arrange for that ship's medical officer to come aboard for a conference. He visited medical officers on other ships while under way, risking being washed into the sea as he traveled by boatswain's chair. On one occasion, when a destroyer was forced to substitute a canvas coal bag for a boatswain's chair, the bottom of the bag tore out just as he was about to land on the deck of a hospital ship. A tight grip on the line overhead was all that saved him.

An example of issues coming out of visits to other ships was that of air-conditioning medical spaces, which Boone favored. A call on the cruiser *Guam* revealed that the dental department was air-conditioned, but the operating suite was not. "I inquired from the senior dental officer of that ship how this came about. He grinned and said by making a set of new false teeth for the commanding officer."[4] In another instance he prevailed on Halsey to send a message to Nimitz:

INVESTIGATION DISCLOSES WIDESPREAD FAILURE PER-
SONNEL SHIPS TO WEAR IDENTIFICATION TAGS AND A
SHORTAGE OF MATERIAL TO MAKE THEM X RECOMMEND
PERTINENT INSTRUCTIONS BE PROMULGATED X[5]

As with the marines in Haiti and in France in World War I, Boone worked with combat personnel and shared their experiences. He was one of the officers who on May 26, 1945, boarded the battleship *New Mexico* at Okinawa to have lunch with Adm. Raymond A. Spruance at the time Halsey as commander of the Third Fleet relieved Spruance as commander of the Fifth Fleet. Boone later told how when Spruance, whose flagship had remained at anchor during most of the Okinawa campaign, offered Halsey the opportunity to tie up to the same buoy, the latter replied, "I am going to up anchor as soon as I relieve you, and I am going to take my fleet and go up along the Japanese coast and rake the hell out of them and I will never stop until the war is over."[6] After lunch Halsey and staff went ashore to call on Lt. Gen. Simon B. Buckner. Boone was impressed by Buckner's hospitality, especially when he knelt on the muddy floor of his headquarters tent, unlocked a trunk, dug under clothes, and produced a pinch bottle of scotch that he shared with the group as he said to his friend Halsey, "I am going to give you something I wouldn't give to anybody else."[7] A few days later Buckner was killed.

As a result of the group's shore visit Boone lost his assistant, Lt. Reuben S. Mixon of the Navy Hospital Corps. While senior officers were with Buckner, Mixon with others explored the island and failed to return in time to catch the *Missouri*'s boat. When a seaplane attempted to bring him out to the *Missouri*, which was under way, it was waved off because of heavy seas. Attempting to return to Okinawa in bad weather, his pilot became lost and the plane drifted into an island cove where Mixon and the pilot were captured by the Japanese. The pilot was eventually released, but Mixon's fate never became known. A fellow prisoner had this to say: "Bob was put in a very small cell next to me. We ate one bowl of rice a day and sometimes none, were beaten severely in some form every day and lots of times severely till we fainted, at which times we were given our only water to drink (we were given a small cup of water to drink every few days), but mostly we fought the guards and took severe beatings to get to water . . . We were hand-cuffed constantly. No sanitary facilities. No medical treatment . . ."[8]

Boone's concern for fleet personnel was illustrated by a statement in his memoirs: "I have been preaching to Admiral Halsey and Chief of Staff and other members of the staff of the Third Fleet as to the relief of ships, like the destroyer *Rooks*, which have experienced so much heavy and serious fighting, and that it was one of my jobs as Fleet Medical Officer to watch for strain in personnel and to advise the Commander, Third Fleet, when strain becomes noticeable . . ."[9] This writer took particular notice of the mention of *Rooks*, since he was serving at the time as that ship's navigator.

Following the death of President Roosevelt, Boone could not help but wonder whether things would have been different if McIntire had not had dual responsibilities as presidential physician and surgeon general of the navy. "Whether Ross McIntire could have saved the President's life had he been right beside him or very close to him at Warm Springs is only conjecture . . . ," he wrote. "I am sure, as Ross wrote me, that the President's death came as a great, great shock to him. I observed to Ross that I knew exactly how he felt."[10]

Boone spent much time on the *Missouri*'s bridge and watched as carrier planes took off for the bombing of Tokyo. He was in a position to be a close observer of Halsey, who impressed him by his sensitivity to the value of human life. Boone took ill from influenza, and the admiral frequently came by to see him. "Whenever one of our planes flying into their carriers . . . would fall in the drink, the Admiral was very nervous, would walk up and down on the bridge until he knew whether the pilot had been safe . . . [When] one pilot or more pilots could not be recovered . . . , he would weep . . . I think he felt he was flying in every one of those planes, having been an aviator himself . . . "[11]

Just before the Japanese surrender Boone played a part described in a letter to Helen on September 2, 1945, now in the writer's personal files. He told how he was the first to land in the Tokyo Bay area on August 29, the day before the military landings, for the purpose of rescuing prisoners. He was in a small group that included Commodores Roger Simpson and Harold E. Stassen, the latter the well-known figure in American postwar politics. Boone described the prisoners' condition and the places in which they were incarcerated as "indescribably *awful*." They had been treated "like swine." Their diet had been rice and grass. His party rescued fifteen hundred men within thirty-six hours.

The details of Boone's experience in finding, releasing, and medically assisting the prisoners are in Boone's report, "Initial Release of Prisoners of War in Japan," a copy of which he placed in his memoirs. An extract of the report follows:

> One of the first buildings entered was what was called the dispensary for the camp. A number of sick prisoners, who were emaciated and ill looking, were lying on wooden platforms without any bedding whatsoever. A room at the end of the building had served as a dressing room and had a number of drugs and dressings on tables and shelves. Otherwise it gave no evidence of being a dispensary as the Americans know it . . . Commodore Simpson, Commodore Boone and Commander Stassen circulated among the prisoners of the camp and into the various buildings to appraise the situation and to inform the prisoners that they were free. The scene was one of wild exultation . . . [12]
>
> This institution (Shinagawa) should not under any circumstances have been designated as a hospital. It had no semblance of a hospital whatsoever. It was a series of unpainted buildings with dirt floors, stinking sickeningly of feces and other human discharges. As a matter of fact the stench of excreta and decaying human tissue was almost overpowering. Patients were lying on platforms made of 12″ boards supported by 2 X 4's which ran around the three sides of each compartment . . . Flies and fleas were everywhere. Many of the patients were suffering from tuberculosis and coughing and expectorating freely. The patients that could not get out of bed had to defecate right on the boards on which they were sleeping. [13]

Boone was responsible for removing the prisoners to the dock, improvising stretchers from odd bits of material, having stronger men help the weaker. They were taken by boat to the hospital ships *Benevolence* and *Rescue*, where they were fed and given treatment. Asked what they would like to eat, they were almost unanimous in requesting ham and eggs—although in their eagerness to swallow solids they promptly regurgitated the food. Pablum, ice cream, and lightly boiled eggs were about all they could handle.

Boone represented the Navy Medical Corps on the deck of the USS *Missouri* at the signing of the Japanese surrender on September 2.

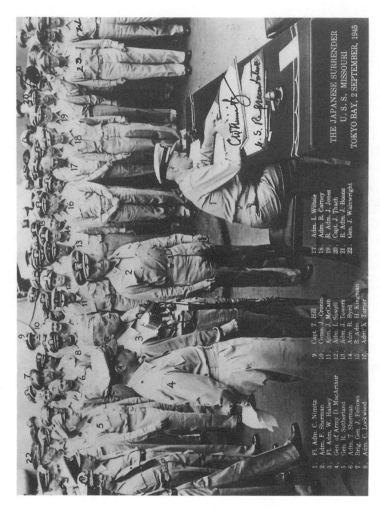

The following labels appear within the photograph:

1. Fl. Adm. C. Nimitz
2. Adm. F. Sherman
3. Fl. Adm. W. Halsey
4. Gen. of Army D. MacArthur
5. Gen. R. Sutherland
6. Adm. T. Sherman
7. Brig. Gen. J. Fellows
8. Adm. C. Lockwood
9. Capt. T. Hill
10. Como. J. Cronin
11. Adm. J. McCain
12. Adm. I. Sowell
13. Adm. J. Towers
14. Adm. R. Byrd
15. R. Adm. H. Kingman
16. Adm. K. Turner
17. Adm. I. Wiltsie
18. Adm. R. Carney
19. R. Adm. J. Jones
20. Capt. J. Thach
21. R. Adm. J. Boone
22. Gen. J. Wainwright

THE JAPANESE SURRENDER
U. S. S. MISSOURI
TOKYO BAY, 2 SEPTEMBER, 1945

As Navy Medical Corps Representative at Japanese Surrender (Official U.S. Navy Photograph)

166

Following the war, just as he was settling into an administrative post on the West Coast, Boone received a phone call on Sunday, May 26, 1946, requiring his presence in Washington. This was five days after Pres. Harry S Truman had issued an executive order authorizing the secretary of the interior to take over the nation's bituminous coal mines during a strike by the miners. Upon arrival Boone was rushed into a meeting with Secretary of the Interior Julius A. Krug; the newly designated coal mines administrator Vice Adm. Ben Moreell; and the United Mine Workers head, John L. Lewis. There Boone learned he was to serve in the dual capacity of medical adviser to the Federal Coal Mines Administration and director of a medical survey of the bituminous coal industry. Lewis welcomed Boone, especially since he had been brought up in a coal-mining area. The Department of the Interior's press release stated that Boone "has been assigned the task of organizing and directing an all-inclusive survey and study of hospital and medical facilities, medical treatment, sanitation, community facilities, and housing in the coal mining areas of the country."[14] It went on: "Since the start of the negotiations between the United Mine Workers of America and the bituminous coal operators on March 12, the health and welfare of the miners and their families has been one of the chief points of controversy . . ."[15]

While Boone formed and led the work of teams representing a variety of skills, he also personally visited mines, hospitals, houses, and community facilities. One day in the company of a local union leader highly critical of conditions in a particular mine, Boone asked the man when he was last down in that mine.

"Oh, me? I have never been down a mine."

Boone retorted, "Then how do you know so much about it? You're going to learn it very quickly," as he tossed him dungarees. The union man refused to go down until Boone threatened to report the case to Lewis. As it turned out, conditions in that mine were better than in many others. The experience taught Boone he should not take the word of any union leader but see for himself.[16]

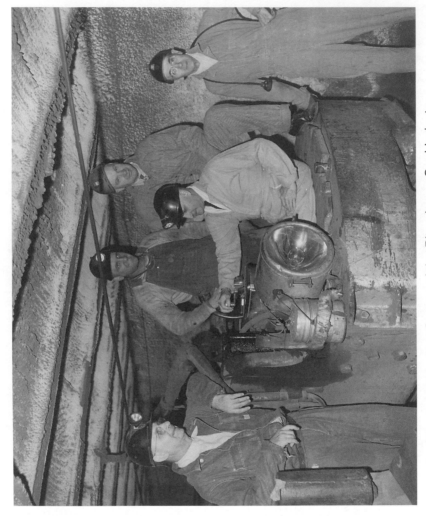

As Director of Medical Survey of the Bituminous Coal Industry

168

Throughout the year-long study, public interest and concern were intense because of the implications the findings might have throughout the economy for management, labor, and public policy. Boone had to contend with pressures from left and right. There was Agnes Meyer, wife of the *Washington Post*'s owner, who after an elaborate luncheon in her home attempted to "indoctrinate" Boone in a concept that he felt had a "socialistic trend."[17] At the other end of the spectrum was Olin West, president of the American Medical Association, who said, "You are going to wreck the practice of medicine in that job."[18] The controversy resulted, of course, from the notoriously poor living and working conditions in some of the mines and surrounding areas, together with the new concept of a welfare and retirement fund and medical care and hospitalization provided for in the Krug-Lewis Agreement.

The study culminated in a book-sized volume on findings, conclusions and recommendations, replete with statistics and photographs.[19] Because the study was the first to deal with the coal industry and its implications for industry in general, it received much attention. Thirteen thousand copies were distributed amid extensive press coverage.

It was only after the report had been bound and distributed that Boone learned how Lewis was reacting to it. He met the United Mine Workers president at a Gridiron dinner in Washington May 10, 1947:

> I stepped up to Mr. Lewis and made myself known to him. He stood up very erect...held my hand and looked at me very directly, then in rather a Shakespearean actor's style, raising one eyebrow and with his characteristic manner of speech, he said: "Admiral, I wish to congratulate you on that very superb report that you have made."
>
> "Well," I said, "Mr. Lewis, I am very grateful that you should be pleased and congratulate me on the report, but I can not other than say that I am surprised that you did so," and he said, "Why, sir?" and I said, "Because I castigated your union so viciously in the report as I had, but I was no less sparing on the operators and the American medical profession."
>
> Mr. Lewis replied with emphasis, "But, sir, the fact that you made your report so impartial gave it great strength and made it

such a superb document."[20]

While the mine survey was under way Boone's name was one of several considered as successor to Surgeon General McIntire. The post went to a younger man, Capt. Clifford A. Swanson, although Boone learned later that three four-star admirals, J. O. Richardson, John H. Towers, and Moreell, had called on Secretary of the Navy James V. Forrestal, asking him to appoint Boone.[21] In later years Boone indicated he had no regret, especially since the appointment would have deprived him of a post he received and relished as chief medical director of the Veterans Administration.

Boone had no sooner completed his work with the Coal Mines Administration and returned to his duties in San Francisco, overseeing all navy medicine on the Pacific Coast, when he again received a call, January 3, 1948, to fly to Washington. There he learned he was to serve as executive secretary to a Committee on Medical and Hospital Services of the Armed Forces appointed by Forrestal (sometimes referred to as the Hawley Committee, named for its chairman, Gen. Paul R. Hawley) to study opportunities for joint use of army, navy, and air force medical and hospital facilities as well as possible unification of the medical services of the armed forces. He seemed unable to avoid becoming involved in controversy.

A month after assignment to the Hawley Committee he received a request from former president Hoover that he also serve as executive secretary of a medical task group of the Commission for the Reorganization of the Executive Branch of the Government, led by Hoover at the request of President Truman. As Boone wrote Helen, "For some unknown reason it seemed that I was being more and more depended upon for this, that, and other kinds of strange jobs."[22] In his memoirs he commented that "there were too many committees studying one and the same thing."[23]

While favoring joint use of facilities, Boone opposed a total combination of army, navy, and air force medical services. His convictions even took priority over his loyalty to Hoover when the two parted company over the issue of creating a Federal

Medical Administration to encompass almost all activities of the federal medical services.[24] Such an administration was never approved by Congress, much to Boone's relief, despite the Hoover Commission's recommendation.

Later while on the staff of Secretary of Defense Louis Johnson, Boone again demonstrated an independent spirit when he testified to Congress *against* Johnson's order to close eighteen military hospitals—an order given without consulting the services' surgeon generals. Boone's forthrightness led to his detachment from Johnson's office because of "lack of cooperation" and to widespread press commentary. The *Baltimore Sun* published a cartoon showing Boone wading ashore from a pirate ship captained by Johnson to join "Admiral Robinson Crusoe (Louis) Denfeld," recently deposed as chief of naval operations. As noted by *The Army and Navy Journal*, within two years during the Korean War, Boone's position was vindicated when it became necessary to reopen, at considerable expense, hospitals just closed.[25]

In the final year of his naval career, 1950, Boone made a contribution to the Korean War after noting at the Inchon landing that it took too long to evacuate the wounded by conventional means. He came up with the idea of transferring them by helicopter from the battlefield to the deck of a hospital ship. Vice Adm. Arthur D. Struble, field commander of the landing operation, "thought I was crazy as hell for even proposing such a screwball idea," Boone recalled.[26] To demonstrate that the idea was practical, he had himself lowered by cable to the deck of the hospital ship *Consolation*, thereby leading to adoption of a new evacuation procedure responsible for saving many lives, not only in Korea but also in Vietnam. To quote a navy source, "For the first time in the history of warfare, battle casualties were able to receive definitive medical and surgical care in a matter of minutes after being stricken. The hospital ship made this possible."[27]

When Boone retired on December 1, 1950, he was honored in many ways. He was particularly appreciative of the parade of marines and this message from the Marine Corps commandant, Gen. Clifton B. Cates: "The high regard in which you are held by

171

Admiral Robinson Crusoe Denfeld Gets Some Company

After testifying against Secretary of Defense Louis Johnson's plans to close eighteen hospitals (Cartoon by Yardley, Courtesy of *The Baltimore Sun*)

"One of Our Own" honored, upon retirement, by the Marine Corps and its commandant, Gen. Clifton B. Cates

the Marine Corps is based on years of intimate association with you. By diligent self-application and devotion to your professional duties, you have given aid and comfort to Marines in war and in peace. By your gallantry on the field of battle, you have been accepted as one of our own."[28]

Boone had the following to say about retirement: "Much of my years of military service in peace as well as in war had their ups and downs and oft were quite rugged, except they brought me soul satisfaction in the main. I knew I had done my best and I was philosophical enough to accept both the rough part of the road as well as the smooth part...I had a most devoted and faithful and steadfast wife who stood beside me always and helped me inexpressibly. I felt the honors that came to me were due to her... We climbed the steep grades together and ran down the inclines hand in hand, singing in our hearts as we went..."[29]

After retirement he was torn between accepting a lucrative position with his friend Moreell, by that time president of Jones & Laughlin Steel Corporation, and heading up the world's largest non-military medical organization as chief medical director of the Veterans Administration. At considerable financial sacrifice, since then-current law prevented him from drawing both retirement pay and a salary from the VA, he chose to continue to serve his country. Among letters received was one from Dick Derby, who wrote: "Ethel and I are inordinately proud of you. I often think how proud T.R. would have been of you. Your standards were his, and there are not many today of whom that can be said."[30]

Upon completion of his four-year term as head of the VA's medical services, Boone found himself in declining health, which brought final retirement from government service in 1955. For the next ten years he devoted time to his memoirs, the principal source for this book. Then, after an extended period of hospitalization, he died on April 2, 1974.

3

It had been a long journey from boyhood in the anthracite

region of Pennsylvania and attendance in the area's schools where he had met the pretty youngster whom he later married, a long journey from the inspiration of the teaching and athletics at Mercersburg Academy to the inspiration at the Hahnemann Medical College in Philadelphia. The decision to become a navy medical officer, particularly, had led him on a path that at the time he could not have imagined.

Life to this point had been guided by a series of coincidences: falling in love with a schoolmate who was to be help-mate ever after, attending Mercersburg because of a stepmother's intervention, pursuing medicine as a result of an uncle's influence, and entering the navy at the suggestion of another relative.

The navy's principal attraction was the financial security it offered at a time when young physicians faced bleak livelihoods in general practice and even among the specialties, which in those bygone years were principally two, obstetrics and surgery. It offered far more than that, however, namely, the opportunity to move out into the world when the alternative might have been to spend a lifetime in obscurity practicing medicine in a small Pennsylvania town.

Totally unexpected, then, were the extraordinary ventures—they really were adventures—that followed. Few Americans, almost none at that time, thought the nation would enter the world war then raging in Europe. Boone could not have imagined that he would go over with the Sixth Regiment of marines and be with the Second Division at the fore of the new national army's encounter with serious fighting, an encounter that in ferocity had not been equaled since the far distant war of 1861–65.

Without doubt it was the young man's war record that set the pattern for what would follow thereafter. He returned from France with far more than the medals he had earned, although for a navy medical officer to win the Medal of Honor was a rarity. Trench warfare, tending men torn limb from limb, himself suffering gas attack and disease, matured him beyond his years. No longer the shy boy from St. Clair, he was a man whose eyes had opened to the world and who had attracted the attention of superiors.

175

Tea with Mrs. Harding at the White House—initiating years of service at the very center of the nation's life—was a logical result, even though it came as a surprise. For eleven years he had an insider's view of presidents and their families as he served them on the presidential yacht *Mayflower*, at the White House, or elsewhere. He shared the joys and sorrows of life during good times and bad. There was the thrill of meeting and working with dignitaries from both the United States and abroad, along with some recreation—riding, tennis, relaxing at the Rapidan. There was the satisfaction of observing patients benefit from efforts to improve and maintain their health. There was the dark side—deaths of First Family patients, the greatest depression in history, empathizing with Hoover in defeat at the polls, suffering the frustration of serving as "number two" under other physicians.

For Boone and his little family the distance from the glamour of Washington to the depressed seaport of San Pedro proved greater than the miles traveled. There was the step-down in responsibility and personal associations, cut in pay, need to fit into a different lifestyle. Not exactly "Siberia," but a shocking experience. Boone nevertheless accepted every assignment—at sea or ashore—as a challenge.

During the war years of 1941–1945 and thereafter, in the nation's efforts to adapt to a peacetime economy, he seemed to have a knack for drawing assignments of a controversial nature—a new position on Halsey's staff for which the admiral had no use, caught in the middle of a conflict between mine operators and Lewis's union, under pressure to adopt economy measures for government medicine, of which he disapproved. He demonstrated he was fearless in telling a superior he should resign, incurring the wrath of the president when insisting that a sick son be isolated from his family, going over a superior's head, lecturing colleagues at the AMA on their obligations to society.

This man became controversial. But that did not bother him. He considered leaving the navy but always concluded there was no substitute for serving as a navy medical officer. How else could it have been possible for him to count three presidents of the United States as patients and six others (FDR, Truman, Eisenhower, Kennedy, Johnson, and Nixon) as friends? He was proud of his record as most highly decorated member of the navy medical service and pleased to know that a building at Mercersburg and a navy clinic at Little Creek, Virginia, had been named for him. To know that Suzanne in 1980 christened a guided missile frigate named *Boone* (FFG 28) would have thrilled him.

Identification of Awards Displayed

Row I

1. Center top: Medal of Honor
2. Left: Medallion for serving on Secretary of Defense's Staff
3. Right: Republic of Korea Presidential Unit Citation

Row II

1. Distinguished Service Cross (United States Army)
2. Silver Star with Five Palms
3. Bronze Star Medal with Combat V
4. Navy Commendation Medal
5. Purple Heart with Two Palms
6. Haitian Campaign Medal (1916–17)
7. Victory Medal, World War I

Row III

1. National Defense Service Medal
2. World War I Occupation (Germany)
3. American Defense Service Medal with Fleet Clasp
4. American Campaign Medal
5. Asiatic-Pacific Campaign Medal with Two Bronze Stars
6. Victory Medal, World War II
7. Navy Occupation Service Medal (World War II)

Row IV

1. Marine Corps Expeditionary Medal
2. United Nations Service Medal (Korea)
3. Korean Service Medal
4. Croix de Guerre with Two Palms
5. French Legion of Honor (World War I)
6. Medal of Honor of the Medical Service (France) (World War I)
7. Italian War Cross with Diploma

Row V

1. American Military Engineers
2. American Legion Distinguished Service Medal
3. Distinguished Guest of American Legion, Los Angeles, 1956
4. Exceptional Service, Veterans Administration
5. Distinguished Visitor, Mexico, 1949
6. International Military Surgeons Association, Mexico, 1949
7. International Military Surgeons Association, France, 1951

Awards Earned by Vice Admiral Joel T. Boone, Medical Corps, United States Navy (Retired) (Photo by Paul Rogers/Stowe).

USS *BOONE* (FFG-28) is a member of the OLIVER HAZARD PERRY class of guided missile frigates. She is designed to improve the capability of surface combatants, defend non-carrier forces, and conduct anti-submarine warfare in conjunction with other sea control forces ensuring usage of essential sea lines of communication.

BOONE is named for the late Vice Admiral Joel T. Boone, Medical Corps, United States Navy. Admiral Boone was born in St. Clair, Pennsylvania on August 29, 1889. He was awarded the Nation's highest military honor, the Medal of Honor, for extraordinary heroism while serving with the Marines in World War I, during which he also earned the Army Distinguished Service Cross and Silver Star Medal as Assistant Division Surgeon of the Second Army Division.

DESCRIPTION OF FFG-28 SHIP'S SEAL

The Crest

At the chief, or upper portion of the shield, are the colors of the Distinguished Service Cross Ribbon, signifying the award of this medal to Vice Admiral Joel T. Boone while serving with the Second Army Division in France. The reversed gold star alludes to the Medal of Honor, this country's highest award. The red cross, a symbol of medical service, bears a fleur-de-lis, referring to Admiral Boone's illustrious service in France. Oak, a symbol of strength, is formed into a wreath denoting honor and excellence. Oak leaves are worn by Medical Personnel of the Navy. The six white stars represent Admiral Boone's Silver Star Medal with five Oak Leaf Clusters.

179

The eagle on a globe refers to the Marine Corps insignia and Admiral Boone's service and assignment with the Marine Corps. The eagle with U.S. shield also reflects Admiral Boone's service to three presidents and his later association with the Veterans Administration.

The Motto

The scroll, its colors alluding to the First Navy Jack, bears the motto of that flag. The phrase, "Don't Tread on Me," reminds us of the United States Navy, and characterizes the traditional rules of engagement of the United States of America. It serves as fair warning to potential enemies as to the lethality of a warship and the naval propensity to prevail in battle against forces of apparently superior advantage.

Official U.S. Navy Photograph
Source: U.S. Navy Official Web Site
http://www.spear.navy.mil/ships/ffg28_hp.html

Appendix: A Monograph Written by Mrs. Calvin Coolidge

THE WHITE HOUSE

WASHINGTON

Suzanne Spends a Night at the White House

One day in October in the year nineteen hundred and twenty-three, Papa Boone received a letter. The letter said, "Dear Dr. Boone: Will you come to Mercersburg Academy to speak to the boys next November fourteenth?" Dr. Boone replied, "Yes, I will come and I will bring Mrs. Boone along, too, because we like the boys at Mercersburg and I shall be glad to make a little talk to them."

When Mrs. Coolidge who lived over in the big White House heard about this she was glad because she liked the boys at Mercersburg and she had two boys of her own there and she thought Papa Boone would have some things to tell the boys at Mercersburg which they would like to hear.

Now, Dr. and Mrs. Boone had a little girl named Suzanne who was three and one-half years old. Mrs. Coolidge had no little girl of her own and she loved Suzanne very much. When she learned that Dr. and Mrs. Boone were going to Mercersburg she thought to herself, "Now is my chance to borrow their little girl and that will be next best to having a little girl of my own." The very next day she said to Dr. Boone, "Do you suppose Suzanne would come and stay all night with me when you and Mrs. Boone go to Mercersburg?" And he smiled and said, "Why yes, I am sure she would."

When Dr. Boone went home he talked with Mrs. Boone and told her what Mrs. Coolidge had said, and then they asked little Suzanne if she would like to go and spend the night with Mrs. Coolidge in the big White House when they went to Mercersburg and Suzanne said, "Yes, I would like that."

After that the time passed very slowly, or so it seemed to little Suzanne and Mrs. Coolidge, but at last the long-expected day came, as all days come, and Dr. and Mrs. Boone set forth in their automobile on their journey to Mercersburg.

After Suzanne had taken her nap, Miss Randolph came to take her over to the big White House. Her grandmother helped her put on her pretty blue coat and her little blue hat with the soft white fur and she and Miss Randolph got into the big automobile and were whisked away. Pretty soon it passed between two large stone posts with heavy iron gates, up the wide drive and stopped before the door of the big White House. Here Miss Randolph and Suzanne, looking very small indeed, got out of the automobile and disappeared through the great glass doors.

Safely inside, Miss Randolph helped Suzanne take off her hat and coat and hung them away in the closet. Then, a great tall man came to play with her. His name was Mr. Haley. You see little Suzanne had many friends in the big White House and they all loved her very much.

In a little while Mrs. Coolidge came to find Suzanne and they all played games and had a good time together until her supper was ready. After that Maggie read to her and helped her get undressed and ready for bed while Mrs. Coolidge went down stairs and ate her dinner.

And what bed do you think Suzanne slept in? Oh, you never could guess so I shall have to tell you. It was the big bed that Abraham Lincoln slept in when he lived in the big White House ever so many years ago, before you and I were born.

After little Suzanne had said her "Now I lay me . . . ," not forgetting "God bless Daddy and Mother and help Suzanne to be a good girl," Mrs. Coolidge gave her a good-night kiss and tucked her in surrounded by her dollies and her books and turning out the lights tip-toed out into the next room and sat down with her knitting and her book trying to imagine that now she had a little girl of her very own.[1]

Note

1. Joel T. Boone, *Joel T. Boone Papers—Memoirs*, Library of Congress, Washington, D.C., Ch.xxi, pp. 46–c, box 46.

Bibliography

Manuscripts

Boone, Joel T., *Joel T. Boone Papers—Memoirs.* Library of Congress, Washington, D.C.

Heller, Milton F., Jr., personal files.

Herman, Jan K., Historian, Department of the Navy, Bureau of Medicine and Surgery, oral history of interviews with navy personnel imprisoned by the Japanese in World War II.

Books and Articles

Adams, Samuel Hopkins. *Incredible Era.* Boston: Houghton Mifflin, 1939.

Coolidge, Calvin. *Autobiography.* New York: Cosmopolitan, 1929.

Burner, David. *Herbert Hoover: A Public Life.* New York: Knopf, 1979.

Daugherty, Harry M. *The Inside Story of the Harding Tragedy.* New York: Churchill, 1932.

Derby, Richard. *Wade in Sanitary!: The Story of a Division Surgeon in France.* New York: G. P. Putnam's Sons, 1919.

Ferrell, Robert H. *Ill-Advised: Presidential Health and Public Trust.* Columbia: University of Missouri Press, 1992.

_____. *Woodrow Wilson and World War I.* New York: Harper and Row, 1985.

Fuess, Claude M. *Calvin Coolidge: The Man from Vermont.* Boston: Little, Brown, 1940.

Giglio, James N. *H. M. Daugherty and the Politics of Expediency.* Kent, Ohio: Kent State University Press, 1978.

Heller, Milton F., Jr. "Dr. Boone's First Battles." *Navy Medicine* 78 (March–April 1987): 22–25.

_____. "Lagniappe." *National Forum* 75 (Fall 1995): 45–46.

_____. "When 'Silent Cal' Used Cocaine." *Yankee* 51 (May 1987): 166–167.

Herrick, James B. "Clinical Features of Sudden Obstruction of the Coronary Arteries," *Journal of the American Medical Association* 59 (December 7, 1912): 2015–20.

Hoover, Herbert. *The Cabinet and the Presidency, 1920-1933*. Vol. 2 of *The Memoirs of Herbert Hoover*. New York: Maacmillan, 1952.

Hoover, Irwin H. *Forty-two Years in the White House*. Boston: Houghton Mifflin, 1934.

McCoy, Donald R. *Calvin Coolidge*. New York: Macmillan, 1967.

Murray, Robert K. *The Harding Era*. Minneapolis: University of Minnesota Press, 1969.

Pusey, Merlo J. *Charles Evans Hughes*. 2 vols., New York: Macmillan, 1951.

Real Calvin Coolidge, The. Plymouth Notch, Vt. Calvin Coolidge Memorial Foundation, 1983.

Sawyer, Charles E., Ray Lyman Wilbur, Charles M. Cooper, Joel T. Boone, and Hubert Work. "President Harding's Last Illness: Official Bulletins of Attending Physicians." *Journal of the American Medical Association* 81 (July–September 1923): 603.

Starling, Edmund W., and Thomas Sugrue. *Starling of the White House*. New York: Simon and Schuster, 1946.

Trani, Eugene P., and David L. Wilson. *The Presidency of Warren G. Harding*. Lawrence: University Press of Kansas, 1977.

United States Department of the Interior. *A Medical Survey of the Bituminous-Coal Industry: Report of the Coal Mines Administration*. Washington, D.C: Government Printing Office, 1947.

United States Department of the Navy, Bureau of Medicine and Surgery. *History of the Medical Department of the United States Navy* 1945–1955, NAVMED P-5057.

Waterhouse, John A. *Calvin Coolidge Meets Charles Edward Garman*. Rutland: Academy Books, 1984.

Wikander, Lawrence E,. and Robert H. Ferrell, eds. *Grace Coolidge: An Autobiography*. Worland, Wyo.: High Plains, 1992.

Wilbur, Ray Lyman. "The Last Illness of a Calm Man." *Saturday Evening Post* 196 (October 13, 1923): 64.

Interviews

Coolidge, John. Interview with Milton F. Heller, Jr. Woodstock, Vermont. September 15, 1996.

McGhee, William, Lieutenant, USN, Medical Unit, White House, Washington. Telephone interview with Milton F. Heller, Jr. August 20, 1996.

Green, Ms. P., Medical Unit, White House, Washington. Telephone interview with Milton F. Heller, Jr. August 7, 1998.

Notes

Chapter 1

1. Joel T. Boone, *Joel T. Boone Papers—Memoirs*, Library of Congress, Washington, D.C., ch. III, p. 6–7, box 44.
2. Ibid., p. 6, box 44.
3. Ibid., p. 6, box 44.
4. Ibid., ch. V, p. 39, box 44.
5. Ibid., p. 72, box 44.
6. Ibid., p. 83, box 44.
7. Heller, personal files.
8. Boone, *Memoirs,* ch. V, pp. 91–92 , box 44.
9. Richard Derby, *Wade in Sanitary!: The Story of a Division Surgeon in France* (New York: G. P. Putnam's Sons, 1919), p. 68.
10. Boone, *Memoirs*, ch. X, p. 37, box 44.
11. Heller, personal files.

Chapter 2

1. Joel T. Boone, *Joel T. Boone Papers—Memoirs*, Library of Congress, Washington, D.C., ch. XVII, p. 112, box 45.
2. Ibid., pp. 101–102, box 45.
3. Milton F. Heller, Jr., copy of handwritten letter, personal files.
4. Boone, *Memoirs*, ch. XVII, pp. 57–58, box 45.
5. Ibid., pp. 61–62, box 45.
6. Ibid., pp. 62, 63, 63a, box 45.
7. Ibid., pp. 94–96, box 45.
8. Robert H. Ferrell, *Ill-Advised: Presidential Health and Public Trust* (Columbia: University of Missouri Press, 1992), p.21.
9. Boone, *Memoirs*, ch. XVIII, p. 62b, box 45.
10. Ibid., p. 69, box 45.
11. Ibid., p. 72, box 45.
12. Ibid., p. 75, box 45.

Chapter 3

1. Joel T. Boone, *Joel T. Boone Papers—Memoirs*, Library of Congress, Washington, D.C., ch. XIX, p. 3, box 45.
2. Ibid., pp. 16–17, box 45.

3. Ibid., p. 22, box 45.
4. Ibid., p. 23, box 45.
5. Ibid., p. 33, box 45.
6. Ibid., p. 38, box 45.
7. Ibid., p. 106, box 45.
8. Ibid., p. 113, box 45.
9. Ibid., ch. XX, p. 3, box 45.
10. Ibid., p. 7, box 45.
11. Ibid., p. 29, box 45.
12. Ibid., p. 18, box 45.
13. Ibid., pp. 21–22, box 45.
14. Ibid., pp. 23–24, box 45.
15. Ibid., p. 24, box 45.
16. Ibid., p. 26, box 45.
17. Ibid., pp. 27–28, box 45.
18. Ibid., pp. 32–33, box 45.
19. Ibid., p. 33, box 45.
20. Ibid., p. 35, box 45.
21. Ibid., p. 40, box 45.
22. Ibid.
23. Ibid., pp. 44–46, box 45.
24. Ibid., p. 46, box 45.
25. Ibid., p. 47, box 45.
26. Ibid.
27. Ibid., p. 50, box 45.
28. Ibid., p. 52, box 45.
29. Ibid., pp. 53–55, box 45.
30. Ibid., p. 55, box 45.
31. Ibid., p. 56, box 45.
32. Ibid., p. 60, box 45.
33. Ibid., pp. 65–66, box 45.
34. Ibid., p. 36, box 45.
35. Samuel Hopkins Adams, *Incredible Era* (Boston: Houghton Mifflin, 1939), p. 380.
36. Boone, *Memoirs*, ch. XX, p. 195, box 45.
37. Ibid., p. 196, box 45.
38. Ibid., p. 198, box 45.
39. James B Herrick, "Clinical Features of Sudden Obstruction of the Coronary Arteries," Journal of the American Medical Association, (December 7, 1912): 2015–20.
40. Boone, *Memoirs*, ch. XX, p. 137, box 45.
41. Ibid., p. 125, box 45.

Chapter 4

1. Joel T. Boone, *Joel T. Boone Papers—Memoirs*, Library of Congress, Washington, D.C., ch.XXI, p. 22, box 46.
2. Ibid., p. 44, box 46.
3. Ibid., p. 125, box 46.

4. Ibid., p. 505d, box 46.
5. Ibid., pp. 505e–505f, box 46.
6. Ibid., p. 506, box 46 (copy of letter following).
7. Ibid., p. 34, box 46.
8. Ibid., p. 879, box 47.
9. Ibid., p. 814, box 47.
10. Ibid., pp. 200–201, box 46.
11. Ibid., p. 202, box 46.
12. Ibid., p, 203, box 46.
13. Ibid., p. 219, box 46.
14. Ibid., p. 209, box 46.
15. Ibid., p. 211, box 46.
16. John A. Waterhouse, *Calvin Coolidge Meets Charles Edward Garman* (Rutland: Academy Books, 1984), p. 43.
17. Boone, *Memoirs*, ch. XXI, p. 289, box 46.

Chapter 5

1. Joel T. Boone, *Joel T. Boone Papers—Memoirs*, Library of Congress, Washington, D.C., ch. XXI, p. 64, box 46.
2. Ibid., p. 66, box 46.
3. Ibid., p. 46a–c, box 46.
4. As told to the author.
5. Boone, *Memoirs*, ch. XXI, p. 47, box 46.
6. Ibid., p. 614, box 47.
7. John Coolidge, interview with author, September 15, 1996.
8. Boone, *Memoirs,* ch. XXI, p. 460, box 46.
9. Ibid., p. 588, box 47.
10. Ibid., p. 101, box 46.
11. Ibid., p. 110, box 46.
12. Ibid., p. 564, box 47.
13. Ibid., p. 734, box 47.
14. Ibid., pp. 241–43, box 46.

Chapter 6

1. Joel T. Boone, *Joel T. Boone Papers—Memoirs*, Library of Congress, Washington, D.C., ch. XXI, p. 813, box 47.
2. Ibid., p. 401, box 46.
3. Ibid., p. 103, box 46.
4. Ibid., p. 247, box 46.
5. Ibid., pp. 957–59, box 47.
6. Ibid., p. 912, box 47.
7. Ibid., p. 936, box 47.
8. Ibid., p. 951, box 47.
9. Ibid., p. 975, box 47.
10. Ibid., p. 954, box 47.
11. Ibid., pp. 857–58, box 47.

12. Ibid., p. 1000, box 47.
13. Ibid., p. 1009, box 47.
14. Ibid., p. 946, box 47.

Chapter 7

1. Joel T. Boone, *Joel T. Boone Papers—Memoirs*, Library of Congress, Washington, D.C., ch. XXI, p. 1141, box 47.
2. Ibid., p. 1180, box 47.
3. Ibid., p. 1221, box 47.
4. As told to the author.
5. Boone, *Memoirs*, ch. XXI, pp. 1226–27, box 47.
6. Ibid., p. 1240, box 47.
7. Ibid., ch. XXII, p. 847, box 49.
8. Ibid., pp. 866–67, box 49.
9. Ibid., pp. 1–4, box 48.
10. Ibid., p. 6, box 48.

Chapter 8

1. Joel T. Boone, *Joel T. Boone Papers—Memoirs*, Library of Congress, Washington, D.C., ch. XXI, p. 482, box 48.
2. Ibid., pp. 51–54, box 48.
3. Ibid., pp. 57a–57b, box 48.
4. Ibid., p. 71, box 48.
5. Ibid., pp. 57d–57e, box 48.
6. Ibid., p. 1075, box 49.
7. Ibid., p. 57d, box 48.
8. Ibid., p. 57h, box 48.
9. Ibid., p. 1301, box 49.
10. Ibid., p. 1445, box 49.
11. Ibid., p. 268, box 48.
12. Ibid., p. 271, box 48.
13. Ibid.
14. Ibid., p. 252, box 48.
15. Ibid., p. 254, box 48.
16. Ibid., p. 449, box 48.
17. Ibid., pp. 449–50, box 48.
18. Ibid., p. 450, box 48.
19. Ibid., p. 454, box 48.
20. Ibid., p. 455, box 48.
21. Ibid., p. 464, box 48.
22. Ibid., p. 464b, box 48.
23. Ibid., p. 550, box 48.

Chapter 9

1. Joel T. Boone, *Joel T. Boone Papers—Memoirs*, Library of Congress, Washington, D.C., ch. XXII, p. 146, box 48.

2. Ibid., pp. 129–30, box 48.
3. Ibid., p. 922, box 49.
4. Ibid., p. 1045, box 49.
5. Ibid., p. 1049, box 49.
6. Ibid., p. 1183, box 49.
7. Ibid., p. 1183b, box 49.
8. Ibid., p. 1333, box 49.
9. Ibid., p. 1436, box 49.
10. Ibid., p. 1435, box 49.
11. Ibid., p. 1342, box 49.
12. Ibid., p. 1344, box 49.
13. Ibid., p. 1350, box 49.
14. Ibid., p. 1480, box 50.
15. Ibid., p. 1475a, box 50.
16. Ibid., p. 1504, box 50.
17. Ibid., pp. 1505–507, box 50.

Chapter 10

1. As told to the author.
2. Joel T. Boone, *Joel T. Boone Papers—Memoirs*, Library of Congress, Washington, D.C., ch. XXXII, p. 196, box 53.
3. Ibid., pp. 272–74, box 54.
4. Ibid., p. 471, box 54.
5. Ibid., p. 474, box 54.
6. Ibid., p. 213, box 53.
7. Ibid., p. 215, box 53.
8. Ibid., p. 525, box 54.
9. Ibid., p. 241, box 54.
10. Ibid., p. 292, box 54.
11. Ibid., p. 380, box 54.
12. Ibid., p. 745, box 54.
13. Ibid., p. 749, box 54.
14. Ibid., ch. XXXIV, p. 178, box 55.
15. Ibid., p. 179, box 55.
16. Ibid., p. 322, box 56.
17. Ibid., pp. 211–12, box 55.
18. Ibid., p. 413b, box 56.
19. United States Department of the Interior, *A Medical Survey of the Butuminous-Coal Industry: Report of the Coal Mines Administration* (Washington, DC: Government Printing Office, 1947).
20. Boone, *Memoirs*, ch. XXXIV, p. 1351, box 57.
21. Ibid., p. 966, box 56.
22. Ibid., p. 1873, box 57.
23. Ibid., ch. XXXV, p. 227, box 58.
24. Ibid., pp. 1106, 1130, box 59.
25. Ibid., ch. XXXVII, p. 298, box 60.
26. Ibid., p. 177, box 60.
27. United States Department of the Navy, Bureau of Medicine and Surgery,

History of the Medical Department of the United States Navy 1945–1955, NAVMED P-5057, p. 181.

28. Boone, *Memoirs*, ch. XXXVII, p. 396, box 60.
29. Ibid., p. 424, box 60.
30. Ibid., ch. XXXVIII, p. 68, box 60.

Index

Somme-Py, 27–28
Souain, 27–28
Spalding, Dr., 141
Spokane, 53
Sports Illustrated, 137
Sproul, William C., 78
Spruance, Raymond A., 162
Stanley Park, 58
Stassen, Harold E., 164–65
Stearns, Frank W., 78, 82, 93–94,
 104–06, 116, 144
Stearns, Mrs. Frank W., 93–94, 97,
 102, 104–07, 116, 144
Stitt, Edward R, 74–76, 78
Stone, Harlan F., 136
Stone, Mrs. Harlan F., 134–36
Strange Death of President Harding,
 69
Struble, Arthur D., 171
Sullivan, Mark, 121, 134
Summerall, Charles P., 28–29
Swampscott, 94, 104–06, 110, 116,
 144
Swanson, Clifford A., 170

Tacoma, 50, 53, 56
Taft, William H., 35, 62, 71, 145
Tennessee, USS, 9
Thiaucourt, 27
Thompson, Houston, 152
Towers, John H., 170
Truman, Harry S, 167, 170, 177
Trumbull, Florence (Mrs. John
 Coolidge), 94, 113
Trumbull, Robert H., 113
Trumbull, Mrs. Robert H., 113

Union Station, 51, 71
United Mine Workers of America,
 167, 169
Upper St. Regis Lake, 98
Utah, USS, 119–21, 131

Vancouver, B.C., 58–59, 68
Van Lennep, Dr. William B., 5–6
Verdun, *see* World War I

Veterans Administration, 56, 174
Veterans Hospital No. 77, 56
Vierzy, *see* World War I
Villers Cotterêts, 25
Virgin River, 54
Vosges Mountains, 18

Wallace, Henry C., 57, 61, 108–9
Walter Reed Hospital, 84–87
Wardman Park Hotel, 47
Warm Springs, 150, 153
Washington Court House, 46, 48–49
Washington Star, 114, 135
West Branch, 137
West, Olin, 169
White Court, 94, 96
White House Correspondents
 Association, 101
White Pine Camp, 91, 96
Wieber, F.W.F., 7–8
Wilbur, Ray Lyman, 63, 68, 147
Wiley, Henry A., 17
Wilson, Woodrow, 35, 40, 81, 90,
 124–25, 127, 129, 145
Work, Hubert, 57, 61–63, 66
World War I, Gondrecourt, 17;
 Langres, 18; Verdun, 18; Belleau
 Wood, 18–24; Marne, 24; Soissons,
 25–27; Marbach, 27; St. Mihiel,
 27; Champagne, 27–28; Meuse-
 Argonne, 28; Landreville, 29;
 Armistice, 29
Wrigley, William, 35
Wyoming, USS, 17

Yellowstone, 53
Yorktown, 145, 148
Young, Dr., 112–13
Young, J. Russell, 114

Zion National Park, 53–54

200